Traditional Chinese Plays

Volume 2

The University of Wisconsin Press

Traditional Chinese Plays

Volume 2
Translated, described, annotated
and illustrated by A. C. Scott

Longing
for
Worldly
Pleasures

Ssu Fan

Fifteen
Strings
of
Cash

Shih
Wu
Kuan

Published 1969
The University of Wisconsin Press
Box 1379, Madison, Wisconsin 53701
The University of Wisconsin Press, Ltd.
70 Great Russell Street, London

Printings 1969, 1972

Printed in the United States of America
ISBN 0-299-05374-1, LC 66-22854

Preface

This book, like its predecessor, is intended to increase the theatre student's knowledge of traditional Chinese acting techniques through a descriptive analysis of the staging of two well known plays, neither of which seems likely to survive relegation in the prevailing cultural climate of Peking. Both plays, although very different in character, belong to an older classical style, called here the K'unshan style, that preceded the popular Peking style theatre but enriched its repertoire and technique.

These translations are intended as an empirical study based on a long personal acquaintance with Chinese acting methods. They are presented for readers primarily interested in performing styles but unfamiliar with the Chinese language. Anyone who writes on Chinese subjects for the nonspecialist reader risks becoming tedious because of the bizarre terminology which romanization systems enforce upon the hapless writer. The old-fashioned Wade-Giles system used throughout this book is most familiar to me because I was taught Chinese by this system, and familiarity dies hard. Moreover, some of the most important writing on China in English has still to be consulted through the medium of this form of romanization. The name *K'unshan* has been used alternatively as a descriptive title simply because it is easier for the Westerner to read and speak, is less semantically complex, and is justified geographically.

The first play in this volume, *Longing for Worldly Pleasures,* was regularly performed on the Peking and Shanghai stages until 1949 and was made especially famous before the Sino-Japanese War through the interpretations of Mei Lan-fang. This famous

actor set a precedent for a rising school of actresses, several of
whom in later years adopted this play into their repertoire. It was
always regarded as rather a connoisseur's piece whose refined,
lyrical fusion of song, dance, and gesture embodied the less robust
but more romantic qualities of traditional classical art. Yet this
little monodrama was not superannuated in any sense; the mimetic
delicacy and sheer theatricality of its composition made a never-
failing impact on the playgoer attuned to stage rhythms.

On two occasions this play has been the subject for analytical
demonstration in my theatre classes at the University of Wisconsin.
I believe that this particular piece offers a revealing study for Western Theatre students and so invited Chang Ch'ung-ho, an authority
on and talented performer of the old school who is now resident
in the United States, to work with my classes over a period. The
experience was rewarding for the students, and the remarks of one
of the more theatrically mature of them are worth quotation here.
"One comes," wrote this student,[1] "to sense that the actress's
movements . . . are refinements of reality similar to Western
mime but the difference is one of value and approach. The actress
does not try to imitate the real as, say, a Eugene O'Neill play does,
nor to escape reality as in the determined fantasy of Western
ballet, nor do without the other elements of communication which
is the serious flaw in Western pantomine; instead she uses gesture
to enforce language and music, not to replace them. . . . The most
interesting aspect of gesture and the area charged with greatest
dramatic impact was the quality of 'stage-worthiness' . . . . One
succumbs to the charm of the elegant line not because it is merely
'pretty' but because it is aesthetically true, an organic co-creation
with the music and words of the play's total effect. . . . The
Chinese actress's control was a comment on our own actors which
was frightening in its contrast. Now that I understand at least
one Chinese play better than I did when I first saw it, I find myself back with a sense of frustration that the few within our own
theatre who really understand the many levels at which gesture
functions dynamically and dramatically have not the discipline to
make full use of it." I would not presume to embroider this
comment!

1. W. McElya.

The second play translated here is an example of a far different kind. In the first place it is an Old Soochow style piece which had not been seen by Peking playgoers during this century until a new version was staged in May 1956 and was enthusiastically received, being acclaimed in the press as an exceptional example in the theatre of the current political-cultural manifesto "Let Flowers of All Kinds Blossom, Diverse Schools of Thought Contend." *Fifteen Strings of Cash,* it was avowed, was a successful example of a revised traditional play being staged "more brilliantly than ever before." (Modesty is not a noticeable characteristic of these kinds of pronouncements in contemporary China.)

In May 1956 I had travelled to Peking from Hong Kong expressly to meet the actor Mei Lan-fang and to see what had been going on in the theatre since I had left China in 1949. A two-hour talk with him in the former Peking International Club ended with his insisting that I go to see the play *Fifteen Strings of Cash,* then being staged at the T'ien Ch'iao Theatre. True to his promise, he sent two tickets round to my hotel that same evening. The play made a deep impression on me when I saw it the next day, in spite of a few reservations regarding the staging. During this Peking visit I prepared notes which are the basis of the presentation in this book, the actual translation of the text being done after my return to Hong Kong.

The following year an English version of the play was published by the Foreign Languages Press in Peking, and if it seems presumptuous to offer my own version at this late date, I do so because my approach is concerned with actual stage procedure, whereas the Peking version is a matter-of-fact rendering into English using conventional Western play format, an entirely literary treatment which differs from my conception. In the first place any traditional playscript of this kind can be only a point of departure, a skeletal outline on which the actor's live performance is developed. Straight literary treatment in this case largely serves to emphasize triteness and banality for Western readers, accustomed to some measure of psychological depth and dramatic progression within the range and quality of the written word itself. In traditional Chinese plays, where language is a physical component of stage rhythm and movement—an aid to the "stage-worthiness" mentioned earlier, rather than a medium of primarily literal communication—the problems of English translation are obviously complex. As I suggested in the previous volume, the translation of any Asian play can at best be a compromise, serving to create an awareness of what constitutes the live stage form.

Assuming literary triteness and banality on a Western level, I have set about the task with the premise that Chinese theatre is essentially to be seen rather than to be read or listened to alone. By standing in front of the stage, so to speak, I have tried to describe rather like an on-the-spot commentator each phase of the actor's performance and all that it physically entails within the time-space relationship. Like every method it will have its critics, and certainly it is not one to commend itself to literary specialists, whether Western or Chinese. It is not devised for them, however, but for those trained to think about a play in terms of physical staging rather than as dialogue on the printed page. As a reasonably accurate if somewhat rough-and-ready record, it can preserve many details that, pertaining as they do to oral traditions, are likely to vanish.

It may be asked why a play revised after 1949 should be included in a series like this. The choice was dictated in the first place by the qualities of theatricality in *Fifteen Strings of Cash,* which I believe justify its being put on record. In spite of the political motives which heralded its revival, it was one of the best examples of a new staging of old plays in a period which, paradoxically enough, seems to have been almost one of good omen in comparison with the dark events of Mao's recent cultural revolution. It is easy to have hindsight, but the time when *Fifteen Strings of Cash* was successfully revived can now be assessed as a politically conciliatory stage of cultural policy aimed at progressive replacement of the old theatrical values, which in the end inflamed recent events in China.

In November 1965 a Shanghai newspaper, under party direction, bitterly attacked a new historical drama[2] played in the old style by a veteran actor, Chou Hsin-fang. Chou had had a long stage career and was popular with Shanghai audiences. He had always been regarded as rather a progressive in theatre circles and had made a reputation for staging historical plays with distinct

2. *Hai Jui Pa Kuan.*

patriotic-political overtones, particularly during the Japanese in-
vasion of China. A contemporary of Mei Lan-fang, he was
schooled in the old tradition but had developed a robust vocal-
gestural technique of his own. In December 1961 at a special
performance in Peking, he had been feted by the elite in commem-
oration of his sixtieth anniversary on the professional stage. Press
photographs of the period show Chou Hsin-fang warmly shaking
hands with a smiling Chou En-lai, who in 1966 was to declare:
"We want to liquidate entirely by this great cultural revolution
all the old ideas, the entire culture."[3] As a result of the hysterical
campaign which was launched against Chou Hsin-fang's performance in 1965, the old actor was personally pilloried and attacked
until, it was reported in the Hong Kong press, he was driven to
suicide in the following year, a fate which other traditional performers are said to have suffered during this period. The tenuous
threads which still bound the past to the present in the old theatre
seem finally severed. Under the circumstances, a play like *Fifteen
Strings of Cash* appears to be a last signpost marking the final
phase of a dying art.

Both the plays translated here were devised as popular entertainment, each having its particular style of emphasis. *Longing for
Wordly Pleasures* is a good example of the more poetic K'unshan
style adapted for Peking audiences, and the version made famous
by Mei Lan-fang is used here. The text, in fact, varies scarcely at
all from the original, except that Northern theatre dialect is used
on the stage as against the Southern dialect of the original play.
Although there are some acting variations in Mei's interpretation,
by and large it preserves the main character of the original. In his
memoirs Mei has noted that old theatre chronicles referred to this
piece as a "fashionable play," meaning that it did not conform
rigidly to classical rules. The theme originally came from an old
storyteller's piece based on Buddhist sources. Such historical
details apart, *Longing for Worldly Pleasures* embodied the true
spirit and form of an older classical style for generations of ordinary Peking theatregoers.

Fifteen Strings of Cash, again inspired by the storyteller's

3. In a speech made in Bucharest, Rumania, in June 1966 and reported
in the *New York Times* on June 19.

repertoire, was written as a genuine K'unshan play even though it does not belong to the most poetically romantic class of the genre and was obviously designed to meet popular tastes. In its present form it might be called a kind of detective story whose melodramatic ramifications, though scarcely subtle, are worked out in the highly expressive and absorbing forms of traditional acting.

The two plays, therefore, both adapted for the Peking stage, represent in sum a transmutation of classical form for the entertainment of the ordinary playgoer and typify a process which has been the life-giving force of the traditional theatre in China, and indeed, throughout Asia.

Longing for Worldly Pleasures (*Ssu Fan*) has been translated from *Su Lu Ch'ü P'u Chih I: Mei Lan-fang T'i Teng* [Su Lu collection of plays: Mei Lan-fang's repertoire] (undated). *Fifteen Strings of Cash* (*Shih Wu Kuan*) has been translated from the edition published by Sheng Huo, Tu Shu, Hsin Chih United Bookstores (Hong Kong, 1956).

Acknowledgments

I am grateful to Mrs. Hans Frankel (Chang Ch'ung-ho) for all her help in the past. Her deep knowledge and sensitive stage interpretations have been a unique source of enlightenment. I must also thank Professor Chow Tse-ts'ung for his constant advice and encouragement while I have been at the University of Wisconsin. Lastly, I must pay homage to the actor Yü Chen-fei, a friend and mentor whose superb stage artistry is a memory that cannot fade.

A. C. S.

University of Wisconsin
June 1969

Contents

Illustrations

Introduction

Introduction

K'un-ch'ü or K'unshan Drama

K'un-ch'ü has been the accepted term for the style of theatre described in this book, but as I pointed out in the preface, it is a troublesome word for the nonspecialist Western reader to read or say. The name *K'unshan* is easier while being just as accurate in the English sense. *K'un-ch'ü* is itself a semantic compromise. *K'un* is from K'unshan, a district in Kiangsu Province whose capital, Soochow, became the center for the artistic development of this style and the training of its performers. *Ch'ü,* which is usually translated in the dictionaries as "songs, plays," is a generic term for a type of verse structure. In order to clarify this somewhat arbitrary classification for the nonspecialist reader, it will first be necessary to say a little more about the characteristics of the Chinese language.

The Chinese language is dependent on a system of pitch variations, which change the meaning of words otherwise identical and which for purposes of auditory comparison have been classified as rising, falling, level, and entering tones.[1] These categories differ not only in pitch but in duration and movement, thus providing a genesis of melodic structure within the spoken language, that is to say, a line structure in the form of successive occurrence of tones in contrast to simultaneous occurrence as understood in our Western conception of harmony. The rhythm and the rise and fall of the Chinese voice thus depend on the innate musical character of the language, rather than on the emotional content of specific verbal statement.

1. *Shang, ch'ü, p'ing, ju.*

The nature of the language has meant that the Chinese have long been preoccupied with the intricacies of metrical structure and invention along with the concomitant elements of rhyme, alliteration, and onomatopoeia in their poetry, song, and drama. Treating words as time-movement units independent of their meaning, poets, musicians, and playwrights used them as a basis for metrical patterns and established formal rules and methods of composition. The formalization of composition, in turn, induced the creation of modal categories, a modal category being a classification which includes several similar modes. The ch'ü was such a category, itself the outgrowth of other categories that had preceded it over considerable periods of time. It was characterized by stanzas with fixed tone and rhyme patterns but lines of unequal length, and instead of the number of syllables remaining constant as in a stricter classical form (*tz'u*) which antedated it, additional syllables were used to provide greater flexibility in composition.

A syllable in Chinese is the equivalent of one written character, so that the number of characters is dictated by the particular kind of rhythm the poet or composer requires. In creating a mode, the poet or composer first selected, or devised, the tone and rhythm pattern and then worked out the words, or characters, to accommodate this pattern. A wide repertoire of modal patterns was eventually created, in this case for songs, and these were given names related to the original lyrical content of a piece. Although the names, because of constant usage, eventually bore no relation to the original association, they continued to define specific metrical treatments that could be used over and over again for given musical dramatic situations. In the case of K'unshan drama there are several hundred of these mode labels (*ch'ü-p'ai*), each a name long divorced from its first literary significance but indicating a particular treatment of a passage to musicians and stage performers.

This explains why time and time again in Chinese playscripts a name is printed before a sung passage in a play. Such a term (*Shan P'o Yang*) is found at the beginning of the second song in *Longing for Worldly Pleasures* and is followed by many others in both play texts translated here. These mode labels specify certain formal treatments from among the hundreds which the dramatist-composer may draw upon and the musician follow in a particular dramatic mood or situation. The use of rhythmic modes immediately recognizable to a knowledgeable audience has been a dominant characteristic of Chinese play construction for centuries.

The romanized Chinese mode labels have been inserted throughout the texts of these translations whenever they occur. Meaningless as they must be to the nonspecialist reader—and their English translation would only add irrelevant imagery—they at least indicate where a change or restatement of dramatic mood is musically required. To help the nonspecialist in another direction, six of the simpler kinds of verse patterns have been reproduced in romanization in the footnotes. Through these, it is hoped that the reader will get a basic idea of the variations of rhyme and meter which are a fundamental feature of every traditional Chinese dramatic text.

It would be difficult to reproduce the musical notation for these modes both because of space limitations and because Chinese notation is based on a rather arbitrary scheme which is esssentially the prerogative of a compositional form intended to be learned orally, memorized, and passed on from teacher to pupil. The set of symbols used in traditional Chinese notation are in fact simple or abbreviated written characters approximating to the notes C, D, E, F, G, A, B, C, D of Western music, although they do not represent absolute pitch but act as a device for associating each musical note with a syllable rather than a single letter.[2] Thus, a single character, or syllable, in a text may have printed against it one or several of the seven notational symbols, indicating in the latter case a vocal prolongation of the same syllable at the different pitches represented by the symbols; in other words, the voice moves through different pitches but in continuous transition. Against the main notational symbols will be found a second

2. In a Chinese scale of the *Kung-ch'ih* system, seven degrees establish a diatonic: *ho, ssu, yi, shang, ch'ih, kung, fan*. The range between ho and fan allows a half tone between the third and fourth degrees, yi and shang. If this scale is continued upward, *liu* and *wu* are used to designate ho and ssu in the upper octave, and there is a second half tone between the seventh and eighth degrees—i.e., the first of the upper octave—following the same rules as the Western scale. Whatever the mode used, the degrees of the scale have the same names. This means that the scale of degrees is mobile and transposable in its entirety in each of its seven modalities, thus shifting position seven times without recourse to accidentals.

system of signs in the form of small circles, triangles, crosses, or dashes; and these indicate different points of stress for the beats —that is to say, the timing of the singing and playing.

The seven notational symbols as they are used in the K'unshan theatre are based on the note pitches of a seven-holed bamboo flute,[3] the principal accompanying instrument of this style. The pitches of the flute provide in theory seven different methods of establishing a scale: that is to say, it is possible to take one or another of these seven notes as a tonic and construct a scale of seven degrees. At the same time, the basis for a series of modalities[4] is provided, and rather in the manner of medieval European church modes, the general characteristics of a modality are transposable to any of the keys. It is this process which provides the rules for composition and versification, and the acts of a play are built up through studied arrangement of the modalities and their keys in relation to mood. The essence of dramatic form lies in their harmonious synthesis.

Singing on the K'unshan stage is characterized by its long notes and an elaborate ornamentation that requires a considerable display of bravura by the performer. The music in general has a strongly plaintive quality, emphasized by the soft and supple notes of the flute, the general effect being one of undulating waves of sound which flow along in continuous pattern marked by delicacy and restraint. Monody and monologue are standard devices of K'unshan performance, and the heightened speech that is characteristic of both monologue and dialogue emphasizes rhythmic pattern and vocal prolongation equally with the singing. The female roles, particularly, make great play with steeply falling cadences as conclusion to a passage of monologue. The shrill laughter of the young scholar is one more unique example of controlled vocal pattern used with great emotive impact on the K'unshan stage.

Articulation and vocalization have their own special character in K'unshan and require the mastering of certain essential princi-

3. *Kung, fan, liu, wu, yi, shang,* and *ch'ih,* which are approximate to D, E-flat, F, G, A, B-flat, and C in Western notation.
4. *Hsiao kung tiao, fan tzu tiao, liu tzu tiao, cheng kung tiao, yi tzu tiao, shang tzu tiao,* and *ch'ih tzu tiao.*

ples. First, there are what are called the five sounds, in which the throat, the tongue, the molar teeth, the incisor teeth, and the lips have a prominent function in the pronunciation of sounds. There are four methods of breathing: in the first, the mouth is opened wide and the sound is emitted freely from the throat; the second involves bringing the teeth together to force through a sound like a whistle; in the third, the lips are pursed, the mouth slightly open, and the sound slips between the lips; lastly, the mouth is open but rounded and the sound emitted from the back of the throat. Next in importance are the four tones—that is to say, the four pitch variations of the spoken language mentioned earlier. For the purposes of the stage each of these linguistic pitch variations has a lighter and a heavier stress; and as the voice must be used against instrumental music, it is necessary to overemphasize to some extent the clarity of the nuances. Another requirement is word articulation, a process in singing by which each word becomes broken down into three: the head, in which the initial is always short; the belly, longer than the head but preserving the quality of sound according to the bar; and finally the tail, which leads the head and belly into the complete pronounciation of the whole word. Lastly, the performer must be skilled in the final of a sound, which is the method of separating a word with precision so that the tail of the word preceding does not become lost in the head of the word which follows. Great attention must be paid to throwing rhyme into strong relief, and the foregoing principles indicate the qualities the actor must achieve in order to master this old lyrical style.

The four principal role categories—male, female, painted face, and comic—represent an abstraction of human qualities and are archetypal in conception. The actor is not concerned with emotional re-creation of personalities, whose specific qualities are in any case taken for granted by audiences, but rather, with acting out these qualities within the considerable demands of convention. The result is an essentially intimate theatre with convention, not illusion, as the guiding principle; formalized acting and symbol replace psychological identification and naturalism in acting, and dance, music, and song are equal parts of the dramatic vocabulary. In the Chinese theatre audiences are never allowed for a moment to forget that a stage is before them.

The History of K'unshan Drama

In a language where metrical device was so vital to musical-poetic composition, dialect naturally became an influential factor in determining the composition of new arrangements and variations of the sound patterns. This was essentially the case with the K'unshan drama, which uses the Soochow dialect common to a district in Central China and completely different, for example, from the dialects spoken in Northern and Southern China. The history of the development of the K'unshan style in its final form is a long and complex one involving a process of adaptation, fusion, and invention within a number of different local styles over a period of centuries. During the Ming dynasty, A.D. 1368–1644, the K'unshan style emerged as the most popular and most patronized of the many flourishing dramatic forms in China, among which it retained a national dominance until the nineteenth century.

It was through its virtues carried to excess that K'unshan drama eventually was compelled to make way for the more robust Peking style, with its simpler language, comic relief, acrobatics, and melodramatic themes. The themes of the K'unshan repertoire tended to be romantic and concerned with such things as the sorrows of lovers and their turmoil and misunderstandings. The subtleties of classical poetic imagery and the need for increasingly ornate language and music led to longer plays, which, while they satisfied the aesthetic needs of an intellectual elite, sacrificed theatricality and virility in the process. The ordinary playgoer bestowed his affections on other performing styles.

It may be asked why a dramatic style whose dialect made it an essentially regional form should attain national popularity. One Chinese authority has pointed out that there were strong economic and social circumstances which determined this phenomenon.[5] By the latter part of the Ming period, Soochow had become a great commercial center, a wealthy city that commanded the bulk of the rice and silk trade, was famed for its weaving, and was a terminus linking the Grand Canal system, China's main transportation

5. Yao Hsin-nung, "The Rise and Fall of the K'un Ch'ü," *T'ien Hsia Monthly*, 2 (Shanghai; January 1936): 63–84.

Plate 1. Chang Ch'ung-ho as the nun in the K'unshan version of *Longing for Worldly Pleasures.*

Plate 2. A stage nun.

Plate 3. The famous K'unshan actor Yü Chen-fei and his wife in a K'unshan play. Mrs. Yü is wearing the nun's dress.

Plate 4. Wang Ch'uan-sung playing the role of Lou the Rat in *Fifteen Strings of Cash* at the T'icn Ch'iao Theatre, Peking, May 1956. Subsequent photographs are of the 1956 Peking staging.

Plate 5. The murder scene: the struggle between Yu Hu-lu (*left*) and Lou the Rat (*right*), played by Chou Ch'uan-cheng and Wang Ch'uan-sung.

Plate 6. Su Hsü-chüan is brought to trial before the magistrate Kuo Yü-chih in the Wuhsi District Court.

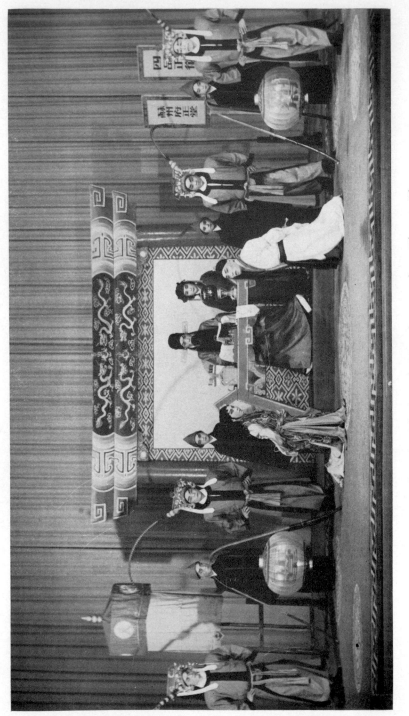

Plate 7. Su Hsü-chüan and Hsiung Yu-lan plead before the Soochow prefect, K'uang Chung.

Plate 8. K'uang Chung searches the house of the murdered pork butcher.

Plate 9. Lou the Rat and K'uang Chung disguised as the fortune-teller.

artery, to the rest of the country. Large concentrations of population and constant communication with the outside world helped to make Soochow a center of fashion whose manners and customs were widely imitated and admired throughout the rest of China. With commercial prosperity went cultural patronage and a climate of artistic achievement in which the performing arts became the focus of a broad stratum of society with means to indulge its leisure. In this connection the point has been made that the public entertainers, the singing girls, the courtesans, and the catamites who flourished in feudal society and were in contact with all levels of the population were instrumental in popularizing their local arts, not least among the merchants who travelled to and from Soochow in this era.[6] A comparison could be made with sixteenth- and seventeenth-century Japan, where the prosperous merchant classes of Osaka and Yedo gave their patronage to the Kabuki theatre. There is a wide gulf between the K'unshan and the Kabuki theatres, but the social circumstances and the ethics of the societies that nourished their respective growths have some strong parallels.

The T'ai-p'ing Rebellion, which led to the military conquest of Kiangsu Province from 1853 to 1863, resulted in the isolation of Soochow and the relinquishing of the last vestiges of fame as a theatrical center. The K'unshan style, already in decline, never regained its former status afterwards, and the Peking style began to replace it in terms of popular appeal. By the beginning of this century the K'unshan theatre had become increasingly neglected, and few of its plays were seen in Peking anymore. The actor Mei Lan-fang has described how during his grandfather's time, 1841–82, all actors began their theatrical training by learning K'unshan techniques.[7] By the early years of the Republic, 1911–49, when Mei was launched upon his own dazzling career, K'unshan specialists were a diminishing body of artists who seemed likely to disappear. At the request of many admirers, Mei studied K'unshan technique and became an active performer.

In the thirties, when Mei moved his headquarters from Peking to Shanghai, he became associated with Yü Chen-fei, who was a

6. Ibid.
7. *Wu-t'ai sheng-huo ssu-shih nien* [Forty years on the stage] 2 (Shanghai, 1954): 125–40. Mei's grandfather was Mei Ch'iao-ling.

scholar in the K'unshan style, as well as a consummate actor and musician. Yü was the son of the distinguished scholar and amateur of the old-style theatre Yü Su-lu, and from his earliest days had been brought up in the atmosphere of his profession. (He once told me that when he was a small child, his mother was in the habit of lulling him to sleep with airs from the K'unshan repertoire.) The partnership of Mei Lan-fang and Yü Chen-fei was a fruitful one. The two first appeared on the stage together in 1933 in order to raise funds for a Shanghai K'unshan Preservation Society. Mei's first appearance after his silence during the Japanese occupation of Shanghai was with Yü in K'unshan performances which ran for four days.[8]

Thanks to Mei's innovations, there was a minor revival of K'unshan drama during the twenties and thirties. The style naturally lingered in its greatest strength in the Soochow area, its original home. The revival of *Fifteen Strings of Cash* in 1956 by an expert Soochow troupe was in itself indicative of a still active tradition. In China during the fifties there was much talk of a new revival of the K'unshan style in common with many other local dramatic forms. A training school was established at Shanghai in the mid-fifties, and Yü Chen-fei was invited to return from Hong Kong, where he had resided since 1950, to direct the new school. Working with him were several teachers trained at Soochow in the early twenties who had been compelled to find other occupations in later years. In October 1961 the first public performance of the graduates of the school was announced and received with acclaim. On this occasion one of the newly graduated actresses gave a much-praised interpretation of *Longing for Worldly Pleasures*.

It is a far cry from this to December 1966, when Chiang Ching, the wife of Mao Tse-tung and once a minor film actress using the name Lan Ping, assumed supreme command of theatrical activities throughout China in her capacity as Cultural Adviser to the Chinese Army. This bitter woman was quick to praise the Red Guard violence which led to the elimination of several old theatre personalities and the cessation of their activities. It is difficult to think, in the light of events since 1966, that an ancient theatre like the

8. Ibid., 1 (Shanghai, 1952): 198.

K'unshan style can survive. The number of artists skilled in its techniques are now in a bare minority, and there is nothing in the turmoil of the contemporary scene to encourage belief that this old art can be perpetuated.

Longing for Worldly Pleasures

Ssu Fan

A traditional K'unshan play

Persons in the Play

SE K'UNG, a young Buddhist nun

The setting is the Sacred Peach Nunnery.

The period is probably Ming (A.D. 1368–1644), but of course, there is no attempt at historical accuracy in this play, designed primarily as theatrical entertainment to which all else is subsidiary.

The musical accompaniment is provided by a seven-holed bamboo flute (*ti-tzu*), the principal instrument; a small gong (*hsiao-lo*); the small, single-skin drum (*tan-p'i ku*); and wooden clappers, or time beaters (*pan*).

In addition to K'unshan and Peking versions of this play, there were other regional versions staged in Hupeh, Shensi, Szechwan, Hunan, and An-hui provinces. Special emphasis was given to the Hupeh-Hunan version as "people's drama" during the mid-fifties in China.

About the Play

Although the performing origins of this play are not recorded by Chinese authorities, it is believed to have been first staged in the Ming period. It is based on a theme from *Records of an Evil Sea*,[1] the title of which is a Buddhist metaphor for a life of sorrow. This in turn was taken from a longer work, *How Mu Lien Saved His Mother from Hell*,[2] which relates a legend derived from an ancient Sanskrit text and famous in Chinese folk literature. For our purposes, it is sufficient to say that this play is based on a storyteller's adaptation of early Buddhist source material. *Longing for Worldly Pleasures* is not a K'unshan play in the strictest sense of the term, belonging to an older regional category[3] which had common artistic roots. The main difference between the two, however, was that the older form had a higher pitched singing tone, and for all intents and purposes today *Longing for Worldly Pleasures* is classed as a K'unshan style play.

The Peking style version translated here became popular during the present century through the interpretation of the actor Mei Lan-fang (1894–1961). His first performances of the play in 1915–16, along with other pieces of the K'unshan genre, helped

---

1. *Nieh hai chi.*
2. *Mu lien chiu mu ch'üan shan hsi.* Mu Lien was the Chinese version of the name Maudgalyayana, who was one of Buddha's chief disciples. The story from Chinese folklore tells how Mu Lien's mother was convicted of the worldly sins of covetousness and greed and sent to suffer the torments of hell. Mu Lien descended to the nether regions to save his mother.
3. *I-Yang Ch'iang.*

reawaken public interest in the old style. In the interests of decorative staging in larger auditoriums under modern lighting conditions, Mei introduced a number of minor changes in the performance of *Longing for Worldly Pleasures,* but these did not affect the basic form and content of the original. His interpretation became the model for succeeding generations of Peking performers, especially for the new school of actresses that arose in the thirties, among whom were some of the most talented of Mei's pupils.[4]

Acting novices used to say that those who played female roles should beware the play *Longing for Worldly Pleasures.* Though not a long piece, it demands the presence of a single actor or actress on the stage the whole time and a mastery of that utter precision and form that only the mature Chinese artist can bring to a part. Poetry, music, and gesture are fused through a sequence of delicately contrived moods in this unique monodrama.

Lyrical as it is, in its own quiet way it is a comment and a social protest. Organized religion has never had an ally in the Chinese theatre, and the little nun's romantic longings are nonetheless effective for their contrasting of stagnant dogma and enforced ritual with the facts of life as we must live it. The old custom of dedicating unwanted daughters to Buddhist temples before they were of an age to decide for themselves puts the audience squarely on the side of the little nun. Her rebellious spirit finds its echo in us all.

---

4. In recent years the actress Tu Chin-fang has been one of the most distinguished exponents of the Mei school, or *p'ai.* She performed in Canada in 1960.

The Nun's Costume

The costume worn in the nun's role has differed in elaborate detail according to the vagaries of well known actors. One of the simplest basic ensembles consists of, first, a long skirt (*ch'ün-tzu*) which covers the feet and is made of plain white silk, pleated at either side with panels at the front and back. These are outlined with a plain blue border about half an inch wide. Over the skirt is worn a garment which is a basic item in any Chinese stage wardrobe, a robe of soft satin known as *shih-shih hsüeh-tzu*. It has a high collar and opens down the front. The sleeves of the robe have very long white silk cuffs, known as water sleeves (*shui-hsiu*).[5] There is a twelve-inch slit at either side of the robe. In this instance the garment is white, but other colors are possible, for the Chinese stage nun does not necessarily shun gaiety in her dress. Over this robe is worn a *seng pei-hsin,* a sleeveless collarless garment opening down the front, patterned in a bold blue and white rhomboid design, and fastened around the waist with a yellow, tasselled cord. This garment is a symbol of Buddhist status and is always worn for that purpose, although there are other versions used in an entirely secular capacity, in which case the rhomboid pattern is not used. Figures 1 and 2 show the nun's costume. Around her neck the nun wears a long circlet of wooden beads representing the Buddhist equivalent of a rosary (*nien-chu*). She

---

5. A standard and functional element of many Chinese stage costumes, these sleeves lend grace and emphasis to dancing and movement. The water sleeve originated in the long sleeves used by women dancers of the ancient Imperial Palace.

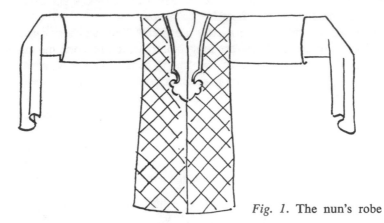

Fig. 1. The nun's robe

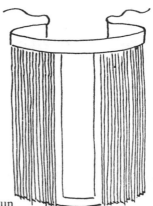

Fig. 2. Long skirt worn by the nun

wears flat-soled satin slippers (*ts'ai-hsieh*) with silk-floss pompons on the toes in a color matching her garments.

In her right hand the nun carries a switch.[6] This article consists of a thin shaft about three feet long bound with silk cord having a thong at the base, while at the top, a broad switch of white horsehair is fixed within a cup-shaped support made of fine, open-worked silk cord. The switch is used on the Chinese stage to symbolize religious status or calling, as well as magical or special intellectual powers. In a more practical function, it provides the impetus for a whole pattern of graceful movements and formal gestures by the actor or actress, and in fact, becomes an extension of the acting form. It is essential to the entire choreographic pattern of this particular play.

The facial makeup is similar to that described for Su Hsü-chüan in the next play, as is the basic coiffure (*ta-fa*), except for a hair decoration (*tao ku chin*) peculiar to this role.

6. *Fu-tzu,* or *ying-ch'en,* the latter being the stage version.

Longing for Worldly Pleasures

*The stage is carpeted and curtained across the rear with an entry
to the left of the audience and exit to the right. There is nothing
on the stage except a small wooden table and two chairs, set at
either side of the table and placed at the rear center. Both table
and chairs are covered with decoratively embroidered satin
coverings.*

*In addition to the switch described along with the nun's costume,
the nun uses two other small properties on stage. One is a wooden
"fish,"*[7] *a crimson, spheroid-shaped block of wood hollowed out
so that it looks like a rather large seashell; it is tapped with a
small, thin stick to give percussive emphasis in the chanting of
Buddhist sutras.*[8] *The other is a paperbacked book in traditional
Chinese style, used to symbolize the printed sutras. A small handbell, another item of Buddhist ritual, is used in the K'unshan version of the play.*[9]

*The nun, surely one of the most decorative novices ever to grace
a nunnery, makes her entry and moves towards center stage, from
which point she develops the action outlined below.*[10] *She moves*

7. *Mu-yü.* The wooden fish, used for percussive emphasis in Buddhist
incantation, was often carried by itinerant monks.

8. The sutras were Sanskrit texts regarded as spoken by the Buddha and
therefore authoritative.

9. The handbell, or *chung,* whose tinkling note is characteristic of
Buddhist ritual, symbolizes the impermanence of all things. The sound it
emits is perishable: "It is experienced but it may not be kept."

10. In the stage directions given for this play, the reader will notice that
the main point of departure for carrying out gesture and movement patterns is center stage. From here the performer moves to the entry and the

21

*with the formalized gait typical of Peking style female (tan) roles.
The feet are parallel and about one inch apart, with the toes of
the first foot about three inches beyond the toes of the second.
When one foot is placed in front of the other, both feet are turned
inwards in a fraction and the whole body is swayed slightly. The
steps are very short, becoming shorter when the pace is quickened.*

ENTRY SONG:[11]

> In former times there was a monk, Mu Lien,[12]
> Who went to save his mother from the gates of Hell.
> "Please tell me how far it is to Ling Mountain."
> "More than one hundred and eight thousand miles."
> I put my trust in the supreme Buddha.
>
> (*As she sings the first line of this, the nun holds her left hand
> up as though in prayer, and with her right hand, flicks the
> switch behind her back to hang down over the left shoulder.
> In singing the second line, she flicks the switch away from
> her shoulder along with a precise turn of the head and grace-
> fully points downwards with her left hand. While questioning
> the distance to Ling Mountain, the actress carries out a deco-
> rative and controlled gesture symbolizing pointing from afar.
> The gestural technique of the female role requires that the
> thumb and middle finger touch in a curve and that the index
> finger bend delicately upwards, with the fourth finger crooked
> slightly above the center of the middle finger and the little*

exit, and to two points or corners of the stage that are directly opposite
the entry and exit, situated at the rear of the stage and to left and right of
the audience respectively. The actor therefore performs the fixed movement patterns at these four points, which form the boundaries of the area
traversed when moving around the stage.

11. This is an arrangement consisting of a stanza of four lines in a
syllabic pattern of seven, seven, seven, eight. The fifth line is the Chinese
version of "I put my trust in Buddha (*Nan wu fo*), Supreme Buddha
(*O mi t'o fo*)," commonly recited by Buddhist priests and worshippers.

> Hsi jih yu ko Mu Lien Seng
> Chiu mu-ch'in lin ti yü men
> Chieh wen Ling shan to shao lu
> Yu shih wan pa ch'ien yu yü ling
> Nan wu fo o mi t'o fo.

12. See p. 15, n. 2.

*finger curved above the center of the fourth finger. From this
basic position both hands, kept about twelve inches apart,
are raised in a graceful, circular sweep to point into the distance, both water sleeves hanging loose and downwards.
During the next line the left forefinger is placed across the
switch, held in the right hand, and thereby making a cross,
which is the hieroglyphic for the Chinese numeral ten (shih);
this is followed by the sign for eight (pa), made by placing
the thumb and first finger together, the two representations
being made to the left and to the right respectively. The
switch is next swung in a circle and held above the head,
which is slightly bowed as though in prayer, while the incantation "I put my trust in the supreme Buddha" is recited.*[13]

The nun next recites these lines:)

RECITATIVE:

It is pitiful indeed to become a nun and have one's hair shorn,
With only a single altar lamp for company at night.
Time passes quickly, bringing old age,
And the springtime and beauty of my youth is wasted.
A humble nun, I belong to the Chao family.
My Buddhist name is Se K'ung.
I have been a devotee in the Sacred Peach Nunnery from
early youth.
I burn incense all day long and invoke the name of Buddha.
When night comes I sleep alone—
How cold and solitary!
(*The first four lines of this recitative, ending with "my youth
is wasted," are technically known as ch'ang shih, which may
be translated as "singing, or reciting the poem." This is a
standard dramatic device for setting the mood of the piece.*

13. In his memoirs Mei Lan-fang has described how he changed this
passage in performance at the suggestion of Ch'i Ju-shan, his artistic
adviser. When he sang the first three words of the incantation, he raised
both hands as though in prayer, then paced in a small circle to center
stage, indicating vexation in his facial expression. The incantation was
then repeated, and the two hands were again raised in prayer before
being pushed forward and outward to emphasize a facial expression indicative of the spirit surfeited with irritation. *Wu-t'ai sheng-huo ssu-shih
nien* [Forty years on the stage] 2 (Shanghai, 1954): 125–52.

The nun is seated for these lines. The "naming" (t'ung ming) follows; in this case, it consists of six lines, but it may vary in length in other plays. Here, the nun describes her identity, family particulars, and other matters, again a standard theatrical device on the Chinese stage. When she recites the first line ("It is pitiful indeed . . ."), she points left with both hands, the switch hanging from her right wrist. At the second line her pointing gesture swings to the front, and the movement is concluded with the left elbow supported in the right hand. The line "Time passes quickly" has three distinct articulations: the left hand points, moves from right to left across the body, and finally the hands are crossed at face height with the palms downwards. With the line "A humble nun, I . . . ," the actress points at herself with her hand, while she grasps the left sleeve lightly with her right hand, the movement being towards the chest, never towards the face. The basic hand position is the same as that described earlier for the "pointing from afar" gesture.

If it seems that excessive emphasis is given to describing "curved fingers," it must be remembered that the hands of the Chinese professional performer are extraordinarily supple, the result of years of physical conditioning. Very subtle arabesques are created through these superbly precise gestures. When the nun recites her name, she holds the switch as though it were a brush for writing Chinese characters and then points with both hands to the right. On the final words —"cold and solitary"—the left water sleeve is flung free; the left palm, facing inwards, is swept downwards from chest to knee; and with a turn of the wrist, the sleeve is flung back a little towards the left. This sleeve movement, known as tou-hsiu, serves as a final punctuation, in addition to being a signal that the actress is about to sing.)

SONG (*in the Shan P'o Yang modal pattern*):
A humble nun just sixteen years old,
Right in the springtime of life:
Already the abbess has shaved my hair.
Every day I burn incense and change the holy water in the
    temple;

I have seen several young men sporting by the temple gate.
One glanced at me and I glanced at him.
Ai, what suspense for us both!
How to be united as lovers!
Then I'd be ready to die in front of the palace of the King
    of Hades.
Let him do anything he likes—
Pound me with a pestle,
Saw me, grind me, fry me in boiling oil—
Aiya, let him do anything he likes:
I've only seen the living suffer.
Who has ever seen a dead man carrying the cangue?[14]
Aiya, let him do anything he likes!
If the fire singes my eyebrows,
I'll only care about my eyes.[15]
If the fire singes my eyebrows,
I'll only care about my eyes.

(*While singing the first three lines, the nun remains seated,
her voice rising to its highest pitch at the words "springtime
of life," as though in emphasis of her youth. In describing
the shaving of her hair, she raises the switch, with the plume
trailing, above her head, while with her right hand she points
to her crown. For the ensuing passage she rises to her feet
and walks as she sings. The words "Every day I burn incense"
are sung at a point close to the stage entry; the phrase
"change the holy water in the temple" is completed near the
exit. When singing about the young men, she mimes opening
a door.*

    *Doors in old China were double, being closed or opened
from the center, where a sliding bolt secured the whole. The
mime that conjures these facts into being was one of the
most characteristic bits of business on the traditional stage.
The gestures used to open a door are as follows: the left hand
is extended palm outwards, while the thumb and first finger*

---

14. A wooden framework which was padlocked around the neck of a
Chinese prisoner, also fettering his hands.

15. A Chinese expression meaning "to think of the present only."

*of the right hand—the other fingers remaining gracefully
curved—are brought into position as though grasping the
bolt, which is then "shot" to the right. Both hands are raised
together in front and drawn slowly towards the actor in a
graceful movement which suggests pulling open the heavy
doors. The actor next steps towards the left with both hands
raised palms outwards and mimes pushing back the left half
of the door; this action is repeated for the right half.*

*This mime completed, the nun glances out and looks right
and left, her eye movements emphasized by the musical
rhythm as she suggests timorous anxiety combined with a
wish to go. Walking towards the entry once more, she sings
"How to be united as lovers"; the line "Then I'd be ready to
die . . ." is taken at mid-stage; and the next three lines—ending with "fry me in boiling oil"—are taken at the entry.
These three lines are embellished with mime gestures at ap-
propriate points. The nun first holds the switch by the plume
in her right hand and suggests the pounding of a pestle;
next, she grasps the switch horizontally as though using it
for a saw; then she turns with it as though pushing a grind-
stone around on its axis. Finally, for the last phrase, "fry me
in boiling oil," the switch is again grasped in its normal position and flicked right and left in two precise movements as
the nun moves from entry to exit. There, a last emphatic
flick suggests that her mind is made up. She sings the following line, "I've only seen the living suffer," while walking
between exit and entry, where she completes the line "Who
has ever seen . . . ." She commences this line by holding
her shoulders with each hand and then folds the switch
around her neck, a symbol of wearing the cangue. During the
last four lines she lifts her left hand to her forehead and
lightly indicates the eyebrow, a gesture (t'iao mao shih) that
is repeated with the right hand. Moving around in a small
circle, the nun reaches center stage, seats herself, and recites
the following lines.)*

RECITATIVE:

When I think about it, my being here is not the doing of
   outsiders:
(*She remains seated as she sings the next lines.*)

SONG:

It is only because my father was fond of reading the Buddhist
    scriptures
And my mother liked to intone Buddha's name.
Every morning and evening they performed religious rites.
Every day they burned incense at the temple and worshipped
    Buddha.
After birth I was sickly,
So they dedicated me to the Buddhist faith
And made me live as a nun.

(*The nun uses only the simplest gestures to accompany these
lines. After the last line, she rises and begins to sing of the
monotony of her daily ritual, emphasizing her meaning with
mime and facial expression.*)

As I intercede for the souls of the dead,
My lips get no respite from invoking Buddha's name.
All I hear are the sounds of bells and Buddhist invocations.
My hand gets no respite from striking the chimes and shaking
    the handbell:
Striking the chimes and shaking the handbell,
Beating the drum and sounding the conch.[16]

(*Beginning at the entry corner of the stage, the nun sings
the line which commences "As I intercede"; then walking in
small circles, she extends the meaning of her song through
gestures. For the ending of the second line, she places both
hands together in front of her breast as though in prayer.
Next she holds the switch in her right hand, and grasping the
plume with the left hand, she moves the switch right and left
as if striking the chimes. At the words "shaking the handbell,"
she raises her left arm with a quick movement of the wrist to
suggest the action; in repeating the line, she uses the right
hand. The nun has by now arrived at center stage, where the
last line is sung. At the words "Beating the drum" the switch
is allowed to hang down from the left wrist; the hands, clasped
together, are moved gently up and down at the left. Finally,*

16. The conch shell (*fa-la*) is used in Buddhist ritual to symbolize the
propagation of the Law throughout the land. In men's ears, it is said, the
Buddhist Law echoes impressively like the sound of the conch, like the
voice of Buddha himself.

the switch is raised towards the mouth and directed sideways,
not immediately in front, to suggest a blast on the conch shell.
 She sings the next line with emotional stress while walking.)
I plead with Hell's authorities without reason.[17]
(*She now walks in a small circle from the entry to the chair*
placed center stage,[18] *and there she seats herself again and*
begins to sing.)

SONG:

I've read the Wisdom Which Has Gone Beyond Sutra com-
 pletely;
The Peacock Sutra I cannot fathom;
The Lotus Sutra in seven books is most difficult to study.[19]
My teacher calls out for me to recite even while sleeping or
 dreaming.
I intone several times, "I put my trust in Buddha,
To-tan-to sa, mo-ho-ti, pan-jo-po-lo."[20]
I say "Supreme Buddha" a few times.
I lay a curse on the go-between.[21]

17. The Chinese hell was a well organized bureaucracy with numerous
ranks through which the sinner had to make his pleas. The implication
here is that the nun pleads to hell's authorities without any reason to do
so, for why should an innocent young virgin have to cry *mea culpa?*
18. The sudden appearance or removal of properties on the Chinese
stage is the work of the stage assistant, or *chien-ch'ang* (literally, "watch
the stage"), who was indispensable in the old-style theatre. In this case,
one of the chairs already on stage has been moved to center stage, the
other being at left rear.
19. The Wisdom Which Has Gone Beyond Sutra, or Prajna-paramita,
is a collection of Buddhist texts compiled in India over many centuries
and dating from the first century B.C. The sutra is largely concerned with
the emptiness of materialism and therefore with the value of all wisdom
according to Buddhist teaching. The Peacock Sutra, or K'ung-ch'iao Ching,
is a theatrical interpolation. No record of this sutra has been found. The
Lotus Sutra (Saddharma-pundarika or the Lotus of the True Law) is
a Buddhist text written about the second century A.D. in India. It teaches
the way to salvation through Buddha's grace, i.e., through the wisdom
derived from direct perception of the truth.
20. Onomatopoeic syllables which have a purely rhythmic function,
but which also represent the Chinese names for the principal Buddhist
sutras.
21. The female marriage broker, often an old harridan, is a figure for
satire on the Chinese stage and often a symbol of immoral practice.

I say "so p'o ho"[22] a few times.
Aiya! I call out that I am helpless.
A few more times I say "to-tan-to."
Who would have thought I have so much to sigh about?
(*Before the nun sits down to sing this passage, she opens a book representing the sutras, which lies on the table before her, the table having been moved to center stage by the stage assistant. As she sings, she slowly leafs through the book. At the line "The Lotus Sutra in seven books . . . ," she stares at the book and emphasizes the line ending with a shake of the head, while a delicate wave of the hand indicates her despair. At the phrase "I put my trust in Buddha," she takes up the wooden fish and taps out a light, percussive rhythm in time with the words and with the line of onomatopoeic syllables she intones at this point. She continues the rhythm until the line "A few more times . . ." and then puts down the wooden fish. Following the final line of the song she recites.*)

RECITATIVE:
The more I think about it, the more melancholy I become.
I'll stroll along the gallery: that's a good idea.
(*On the word "gallery" she stands, picks up the switch, which has lain on the table during her song, and completes the last line while moving away from the chair. Arriving front stage she pauses and mimes opening a door. There was always a wooden threshold several inches high, over which one had to raise one's feet when entering or leaving; and after opening the temple door, the nun "steps over the threshold" by lifting her right foot and then placing it squarely on the ground as she lifts her left foot slightly to the rear before bringing it into position. The action completed, the nun walks around in a circle while singing the following two lines.*)

SONG:
I'll stroll along the gallery to dispel my melancholy.
I'll stroll along the gallery to dispel my melancholy.
(*She mimes opening a door, enters the Hall of the Lohans,[23] and recites the following lines.*)

22. The Chinese version of the Sanskrit word *svaha*, used in terminating Buddhist incantations and comparable to the Western "amen."
23. *Lohan* is the Chinese word for the Sanskrit *Arhat*, meaning one of

RECITATIVE:

> Look at those Lohan statues on either side of the gallery,
> how solemn they seem.
> (*She next begins to sing a passage in the K'u Huang T'ien
> modal pattern, in which she describes, both through words
> and gestures, the appearence of the seven Lohan statues
> lining the hall.*)

SONG:

> All I can see are two rows of Lohan statues.
> Don't they look foolish?
> One hugs his knees and sits motionless
> As though he were thinking of me.
> One supports his scented cheeks in his hands
> As though he were longing for me.
> One leers at me with half-open eyes.
> Only the Lohan with the calico sack laughs at me—
> Laughs at me because time wastes away;
> As time passes, who will be willing,
> Who will be willing to marry me,
> An aged hag?
> The Lohan who conquers the dragon is angry with me.
> The Lohan who subdues the tiger loathes me.
> The great saint with the long eyebrows worries about me
> And thinks what will become of me when I get old.
> (*She continues her song in the Hsiang Hsüeh Teng modal
> pattern.*)
> Altar lamps are unsuitable as decorated candles for the bridal
> chamber.
> A nunnery kitchen is unsuitable as a reception hall for choos-
> ing a son-in-law.
> A temple with bells and drums is unsuitable as a terrace for
> awaiting a husband's return.
> Straw mats cannot replace soft, flower-embroidered bedding.
> I am a graceful, beautiful woman,
> Ai, not a hardy man.
> Why is my waist bound with a yellow cord?

the chief disciples of Buddha. A Lohan is one who has attained Nirvana,
the release from the limitations of existence which is the supreme goal of
Buddhism.

Why do I wear patched clothes?
I see other people walking together as man and wife,
Happy and free, wearing silk and brocade.
(*Exclaims.*)
Aiya, heaven above!
(*Sings.*)
I cannot help myself: my heart burns as though on fire.
I cannot help myself: my heart burns as though on fire.
(*At the words "All I can see" the nun holds the switch behind her back, then swings it forward to point from left to right for "two rows of Lohan statues." Lifting her hand to her eyebrows for the words "Don't they look foolish?" and allowing the switch to hang loosely from her wrist, she slowly turns in a small circle to face the entry corner, her body slightly inclined as she glances from side to side. At the words "One hugs his knees . . ." she walks to the entry and squats, arms crossed, hands palms down and placed on on her knees. As she sings "One supports his scented cheeks . . .," she rises, walks to the exit corner, and again squats, supporting her chin lightly on one hand. At the final "me" in the following line, she turns her face slightly towards the right, holding one hand in front of her and one behind, with palms outward, as she suggests concealed embarrassment with a single glance at the stage entry. On the line "One leers at me . . ." she walks towards the entry, first performing the gesture known as fan yün-shou, in which both hands are rubbed lightly together to the right and then, with fingers outstretched, gently drawn before each eye from the nose to the outer corner. The nun finishes singing the line as she arrives at the entry. At the beginning of the line "Only the Lohan . . .," she walks from entry to exit; on the words "laughs at me" she returns to the entry using a step (yün-pu) in which the left foot, placed apart from the right foot, is drawn up obliquely three times and the movement is then repeated on the alternate foot. She claps her hands upon arriving at the entry, then moves quickly to center stage on the words "Laughs at me because time wastes away." During the repetitive "Who will be willing," she holds her hands open with upturned palms and thumbs bent to the middle*

fingers, a gesture called t'an shou. At the line "The Lohan who conquers the dragon . . ." the nun stands center stage and points downwards, first with the left, then with the right hand, her eyes following each gesture and hatred expressed on her face. She turns her back on the audience for the line "The great saint . . ." and faces rear center stage. The switch is flicked upwards with the right hand, and the left water sleeve is simultaneously flicked in the same direction as the nun turns to face the audience again, pointing first at her chest and then reverting to the t'an shou hand gesture. The pointing is done with the left hand, the thumb and middle fingers touching in a curve, the fourth finger bent above the center of the middle finger, and the little finger in turn curved above the fourth finger. The pointing hand is held away from the body with the palm upturned and then gracefully turned inwards towards the breast, during which the right hand holds the left sleeve. Using the same pointing gesture, the nun counts the seven Lohans.

When the nun begins to sing in a new modal pattern on the line "Altar lamps are unsuitable . . .," she is at center stage. She walks towards the entry for the line "A nunnery kitchen . . .," then back to center stage for "A temple with bells . . .," returning to the entry for the last portion of this line, then back to center stage again for "Straw mats cannot replace . . . ." During this singing and promenading a number of gesture patterns are performed. At the words "Altar lamps" the nun points to the stage entry, and for the words "decorated candles . . ." she crosses her left hand over the switch, which she holds in her right hand, the gesture being made to the left and followed up with pointing at the stage exit. As she turns and walks towards the entry, she flicks the switch across her left shoulder to the rear, then squats to face the exit. On the line "A temple with bells . . ." she rises, pointing first to the right, then to the left; she next shakes her head from side to side, retreats three paces, walks forward three paces, and performs the gesture of looking into the distance as she faces the exit. The right hand is raised to head height and the water sleeve flicked upwards to the rear with a quick circular turn of the wrist. While she sings

"Straw mats . . .," she holds the switch tail downwards and swings it in a circular motion to indicate matting on the ground; when she reaches the words "soft, flower-embroidered bedding," she slowly sinks downwards to a kneeling posture, holding the switch at both ends and moving it sideways across the body.

For the line "I am a graceful, beautiful woman," the nun is at the stage entry, the switch in her right hand with the tail grasped by the left hand; in this position she sways rhythmically three times from the waist as she simultaneously steps three paces backwards. This is symbolical of a girl's putting on courting airs. On the word "Ai," she flings both water sleeves forward and outward with the circular wrist movement; and this is followed by three steps sideways from right to left utilizing the broader masculine gait, the body being inclined backwards slightly from the waist and both hands raised to face height at the front, the right hand slightly in front of the left, water sleeves folded in position over the fingers and partially concealing the face. The nun lifts the tasselled cord she is wearing at the words "Why is my waist bound . . .," and with the line "Why do I wear . . .," she inclines her body a little to one side from the waist with her hands crossed on her chest; one elbow is drawn in to the body and the other slanted upwards at face level to follow the general line of the main posture. During the words "walking together as man and wife," she raises both hands palms upwards, index fingers extended, and then moves them in and out from the body in time with two or three paces taken backwards. For "wearing silks and brocades" she crosses both hands on her chest, elbows at the same level. Finally, as she sings "Aiya, heaven above!" the nun circles around to return to center stage, where, on the line "I cannot help myself," she raises both hands, palms upturned, to chest height, and then raises them lightly to her forehead, the process being repeated as the line is repeated.

Up to this point the song and gesture of the nun have conveyed three major changes of mood: indignation with her lot, a fierce conflict of mind, and lastly, the decision to renounce her way of living. In the next and final passage her

tension, boredom, hatred of religious dogma, and return to
worldly pleasures are portrayed through her mime, song, and
gesture. From the center stage the nun now recites the fol-
lowing lines:)

RECITATIVE:

Today the abbess and all the other nuns have gone out.
I could run away down the mountain.
Who knows, it may be a chance.
That's the way, that's the way.
(*On the words "Today the abbess . . .," the nun clasps both*
hands in front of her breast, right fist doubled in the left
palm, and moves them backwards and forwards two or three
times to symbolize respectful salutation. At the words "have
gone out" she points to the entry, and at "I could run away
down the mountain," to the exit. For "Who knows, it may
be a chance," she lifts both hands, index fingers extended;
next, she claps her hands once, first right then left, for the
repeated "That's the way." She then sings in the Feng Ch'ui
Ho Yen Sha modal pattern.)

SONG:

I'll tear my nun's robe to pieces.
I'll bury the Buddhist scriptures.
I'll throw away the wooden fish.
I'll cast aside the cymbals.
Not for me to learn how to become a female exorcist;
Not for me to learn how to become a Bodhisattva of the
    Southern Seas.[24]
In the deep night I sleep alone;
When it is time to rise I sit alone.
Is there anybody as lonely and miserable as I?
Why should my hair be shaved in this way?
I hate, I simply hate the lies the monks tell the laymen:

---

24. The reference here is to Kuan-yin, the Goddess of Mercy widely
revered throughout China; she represented the feminine aspect of
Avalokitsevara, the Buddhist Lord of Compassion. Kuan-yin, "she who
hears prayers," was a Bodhisattva—that is, one who, by the tenets of
Mahayana Buddhism, had attained enlightenment but had renounced
Nirvana in order to aid humanity in its earthly travail. In China, Kuan-yin
was frequently depicted as clothed in white and bearing a child in her arms.
She was worshipped especially by women, including those who wished to
become mothers.

How can there be a Buddha of the Tree in the Garden of
the World?

How can there be a Buddha Bright in Every Branch and
Leaf?

How can there be a Buddha of Rolling Sands on the Banks
of Rivers and Lakes?

How can there be eighty-four thousand Supreme Buddhas?

After this I want to get away from bell tower and temple.

I want to go down the mountain and seek a lover.

I don't care if he beats me, scolds me, laughs at me, maligns
me:

I've made up my mind I don't want to become a Buddha.

I will not recite "Supreme Buddha" and the Wisdom Wnich
Has Gone Beyond!

RECITATIVE:

Good, how lucky I have escaped and come down the mountain.

SUNG FINALE (*in the Wei-sheng modal pattern*):

I only want to have a child.

I shall die of happiness.

(*For the line "I'll tear my nun's robe to pieces," the nun
inclines her body slightly to one side, as she flicks the switch
upwards with the right hand and the water sleeve upwards
with the left hand. At the words "I'll bury the Buddhist
scriptures," she walks over to the table, and putting the
wooden fish aside at the right, she closes the open book. For
"I'll cast aside the cymbals," she faces the audience and mimes
going through a door and closing it behind her.[25] To do this
she first mimes crossing the threshold and turns towards the
"door." Stepping inside with the right foot, she draws the
left-hand portion of the door shut with her right hand and
the right portion with her left hand and then "shoots" the
bolt.*

This done, the nun, with downcast eyes, circles the stage

25. In the Chinese original the last syllable for "cast aside the cymbals"
(*tiu liao nao po*) is prolonged and drawn out to an exceptional degree.
This particular feature of the play's musical construction, known as *lang-
t'ou*, is based on a rhythmic pattern of one accented and one light beat
(*i-pan, i-yen*), the sung syllable being carried on for three or five beats
by the drummer, who is the time beater in the stage orchestra.

singing. On the line "Not for me to learn . . .," she walks in a circle to the entry and returns to the exit corner on the words "female exorcist." She sings the next line while walking in a circle to center stage, taking the following two lines at center stage. "Is there anybody as lonely . . ." is taken at the exit and "Why should my hair be shaved . . .," at the entry. At the end of this the elongated rhythm previously described is again used. While the nun circles the stage, she uses the following gestures. At the phrase "Bodhisattva of the Seven Seas," she stands slightly to the right of center stage and flicks the switch up and down in the direction of the audience; on the final word of the line she kneels with her hands placed one over the other at her right. She uses the hand gesture for sleeping with the words "In the deep night I sleep alone," while when she turns to face the audience with the words "When it is time to rise," she opens her hands, placed one before the other, with a scissor motion across the face, and follows this by making a gesture of sitting down. On the words "Why should my hair be shaved . . .," she rubs the palms of both hands lightly in a circular motion at face level to the right.

The line "I hate . . ." is taken at the entry corner, and the next four lines—those beginning "How can there be"— are taken alternately at the exit, then at the entry. These four references to Buddha provide points for embellishing the singing with gesture patterns. At the first description the nun raises both hands and poses with the right hand held high and the left pointing to the ground. For the second description she flicks the left water sleeve above her head and sweeps the switch forward in her right hand. For the third description she kneels with one hand placed over the other at her right. In the last pose the nun kneels once more with the switch held diagonally across her breast, the left hand raised against the shaft of the switch and the palm of the hand to the right.

In the concluding portion of the song, the words "After this I want to get away" are taken at mid-stage, and the line as a whole is terminated at the exit. The line "I've made up my mind . . ." is taken at the entry, the words "I will not recite 'Supreme Buddha' " at the exit, and "Wisdom Which Has Gone Beyond" at the entry. There is thus a constant flow of movement between the two extremes of the stage while the singing is going on. On the words "bell tower" the nun points deliberately with the switch first at the entry, then the exit, the singing of these words being in slow tempo. She sings "I want to go down the mountain" with rhythmic prolongation of the final syllable, and during this time, moves from exit to entry performing a number of gestures. First, she swings the switch to the left and then to the right. Then, with the shaft in her right hand and the tail in her left, the performer moves sideways across the stage using a step called ts'o-pu, in which the legs are crossed with the feet placed together and exceptionally short steps are used to propel the body along. Arrived in this fashion at the entry corner, the nun kneels, holding the switch above her head with both hands, and from this position, turns her head towards the exit. At the words "seek a lover" she rises to point at the audience; at "beats me" she flicks the switch towards the audience, pointing at herself for the remainder of the line. For the final line ("Wisdom Which Has Gone Beyond") she again uses the ts'o-pu step, commencing with the right foot and this time moving from entry to exit, where she again kneels to take her pose, her head now facing the entry. These two passages of quick, agitated steps symbolize the hasty escape of the nun down the mountain path, the prolonged rhythms used allowing ample time for perfectly formed gestures.

On reciting "Good, how lucky . . .," the nun points to a place high above the entry. She returns to center stage to sing the finale. During the singing she holds the switch by the tail with her left hand over her right arm, which is held with the hand open as though suggesting the height of a child from the ground. On the words "I shall die of happiness," the nun takes three steps towards the entry corner, claps her hands three times with a smile for the audience, and makes her exit.)

THE END

Fifteen Strings of Cash

Shih Wu Kuan

A traditional K'unshan play

Persons in the Play

YU HU-LU, a bibulous pork butcher
CH'IN KU-HSIN, his old neighbor
SU HSÜ-CHÜAN, Yu Hu-lu's stepdaughter
LOU THE RAT, a gambler and a rogue
HSIUNG YU-LAN, a merchant's apprentice
KUO YÜ-CHIH, Magistrate of Wuhsi
K'UANG CHUNG, Prefect of Soochow
CHOU CH'EN, Governor of Kiangsu
NEIGHBORS A, B, C, AND D
TWO COURT RUNNERS
FOUR COURT ATTENDANTS
FOUR EXECUTIONERS
JAILER
ASSISTANT TO K'UANG CHUNG
NIGHT DUTY OFFICER AT THE GOVERNOR'S OFFICIAL RESIDENCE
CAPTAIN OF THE GUARD AND FOUR GUARDS
HEADMAN

The action takes place as follows:

Scene 6   The street near Yu Hu-lu's house
           The interior of Yu Hu-lu's pork shop
Scene 7   At the foot of Mount Hui near the Eastern Peak Temple
           The interior of the Eastern Peak Temple
           Outside the temple
Scene 8   The exterior of the Soochow prefectural court
           The interior of the court

The changes of scene are achieved by the use of a second curtain. The introduction of this curtain and of the settings described in the text are typical of Chinese stage practice since 1949.

The time of the action is probably intended to be late seventeenth century, but as with the preceding play, there is no attempt at historical accuracy.

The principal instruments used for the musical accompaniment of this play are the bamboo flute (*ti-tzu*), the single-skin drum (*tan-p'i ku*), the time-beating clappers (*pan*), the stringed instrument called the *hu-ch'in,* and the large, barrel-shaped drum (*t'ang ku*), used for effects offstage.

The cash, the monetary unit which inspires the title of this play and the motive for the plot, was a copper coin worth one-twentieth of a penny. Each cash had a square hole punched in the center for threading on strings, which provided a convenient means of carrying quantities of the coin around.

About the Play

The tale that provided the theme for this play first appeared in a collection of storytellers' prompt books[1] published during the thirteenth century A.D. and reappeared in a later collection dated 1627.[2] It was from the latter version that the K'unshan play was first devised and performed during the seventeenth century, although the play was somewhat different from the original story, being longer and more complex in the ramifications of plot. (Theatregoers of those days liked to be given a good run for their money.) According to Chinese authorities,[3] by the end of the nineteenth century only certain scenes from the play were still performed, notably those featuring a rascally character nicknamed Lou the Rat. This part was made famous by the talented Soochow comic actor Yang San, who was a favorite with Peking audiences and in his day perpetuated an older tradition for a new generation.[4] During the present century the play disappeared from the Peking stage and was unknown to Northern playgoers, being staged only by troupes in the Soochow area. Even there, it was becoming less known in the repertoire.

In May 1956, a new version of *Fifteen Strings of Cash* was staged in Peking by the Chekiang K'un-ch'ü Drama Troupe. It was performed in the original Soochow dialect with the text pro-

1. *Ching-pen t'ung-su hsiao-shuo* [Popular stories of the capital].
2. *Hsing-shih heng-yen* [Stories to awaken men].
3. "Chronicle," *Chinese Literature*, 1957, no. 5.
4. Mei Lan-fang gives a description of Yang in the role of Lou the Rat in his memoirs. *Wu-t'ai sheng-huo ssu-shih nien* [Forty years on the stage] 1 (Shanghai, 1952): 34.

jected on a screen at the side of the stage for the Peking dialect speaking audiences, in itself a comment on the ancillary nature of literary statement within the acting form. Officially proclaimed as an example of the policy of "weeding out the old and letting the new emerge," this fresh version of a nearly forgotten play certainly scored a success with the theatregoing public.

The story of the play is briefly as follows. A bibulous pork butcher returns home one night very drunk and carrying fifteen strings of cash loaned him by a women relative to help start up his bankrupt shop again. Before stumbling to bed, he informs his pretty stepdaughter that he in fact received the money for her purchase price as a slave girl. Believing his drunken jesting, the terrified daughter runs away in the night to seek safety with an aunt in a distant town. After her flight, Lou the Rat—rogue, gambler, and petty thief—seeing lights in the pork shop and the door ajar, enters to find the butcher snoring on his bed and his half-concealed money visible beneath the pillow. In trying to make off with it, the Rat awakens the tipsy sleeper, a struggle ensues, and the pork butcher is killed with his own meat chopper.

The next morning the neighbors find the corpse, and Lou the Rat, who is among them, cunningly directs suspicion toward the missing daughter. The watch are called out, and the neighbors join in the search. The daughter is discovered on the highway in the company of a merchant's apprentice sent to buy goods in the town for which the girl is also headed. Unfortunately for the apprentice, the purchase money he carries totals exactly fifteen strings of cash. The young couple are thrown into jail right away and condemned to death by a stupid circuit judge who requires no other proof than the circumstantial evidence available. In despair, the young couple appeal to the local prefect, who has been ordered to supervise the execution but is noted for his fairmindedness. After listening to their full story, he obtains reluctant permission from his immediate superior to conduct an investigation. Disguised as a fortune-teller, he tracks down Lou the Rat to a country temple and in a classic scene obtains all the evidence he requires through a piece of smart detective work. The murderer is arrested and brought to trial, while the wronged young couple are pardoned, rewarded, and set free.

The revised version of this old play has eliminated many of the side issues which were introduced by the playwright to give the old-style audiences value for their money; and the main theme has been pruned of a more involved plot line which once occupied twenty-nine scenes. Old phraseology has frequently been replaced by colloquial speech, a concession to the modern playgoer, who no longer has the connoisseur's knowledge of traditional dramatic conventions that his predecessors had. The conflict between the officials in the play has been heightened in terms of elemental black and white, and the triumph of righteousness over corrupt officialdom brought out as sharply as possible.

The 1956 production of the play was hailed with a spate of the party verbiage and political moralizing that has become so tediously repetitious in China. "*Fifteen Strings of Cash* was written in feudal times," wrote one critic; "it clearly exposed the crimes of that barbarous, decadent society and extolled K'uang Chung (the magistrate) for fighting for the rights of good citizens even at considerable risk to himself. The realist significance of this historical play lies in the fact that its artistic imagery opens men's eyes and helps them to overcome the feelings and pernicious ideas which Kuo Yü-chih (the stupid judge) possessed and which they inherited from the old society, and encourages them to adopt an attitude like K'uang Chung's to their work, life, and fellow men."[5]

It is true that this play lays it on with a trowel when contrasting official ineptitude and fair dealing in old China, and no one who has had experience of Chinese governmental corruption and nepotism in the past would deny the justification for dramatic satire of this kind. The general administrative body of the old provincial civil service—the prefects and magistrates—collected revenue, maintained order, dispensed justice, conducted literary examinations, and upheld ethical codes. This multiplicity of functions provided an obvious source for theatrical exploitation of human virtues and failings in the age-old conflict of the people versus authority. But making the acting deed suit the political word can overdo description of plots that, for stage purposes, are already contrived. The fact remains that for the unprejudiced Chinese playgoer, the real appeal of this play lay in the performance of the actor playing Lou the Rat, as the playwright intended: this rogue

5. "Chronicle," *Chinese Literature*, 1957, no. 5.

provided the motive for the dramatic rhythm of the play. *Fifteen Strings of Cash* is a vehicle for the art of the Chinese comic actor at its most subtle and sustained level, and no amount of political wishful thinking makes it otherwise. Wang Ch'uan-sung, the veteran Soochow actor who played Lou the Rat in the 1956 Peking revival, gave a brilliant performance in the best tradition of the masters and of a kind that will probably not be seen again. His interpretation of every shade of crafty stealth, sly roguery, and downright evil through minute gesture and facial expression was a tour de force that made the greatest masters of Western mime seem mere amateurs.

In the traditional Chinese theatre, the comic role (*ch'ou*) has a dramatic function that cannot be dismissed in terms of mere farce or knockabout, although both have their place. The traditional Chinese comic actor functions on the assumption that all the world really is a stage and that therefore anything is valid in a play. He is an integral part of a regular theatre company and is not relegated to another kind of stage show, like our Western music hall, which has come to be regarded as something quite distinct from legitimate theatre and acting. The comic actor is regarded, not as operating within a lower scale of artistic values, but as a professional whose accepted place is the serious stage.

Like all other Chinese actors, he must undergo a long and rigorous training. He uses a standardized makeup consisting of a white patch on the center of his face, embellished with various black markings which vary from role to role but are standard to a specific character. This seemingly ludicrous makeup indicates not only simple comedy or knavery; it can also symbolize evil or tragedy in a deeper sense. The Chinese comic player may be the clown pure and simple, the essence of whose performance lies in what he says or does, or he may be the master of wit and improvisation who does not hesitate to offer his confidences to the audience, with whom he remains in constant and intimate communication. He is the authorized commentator, the butt, a psychological safety valve, the inner contradiction in us all. He has frequently been the vehicle for satire in a stringently controlled community where freedom of social comment was not acceptable. Roles such as a stupid, corrupt official or a lecherous monk enable him to mock bureaucracy or jibe at religion. The shrewish mother-in-law or the scheming go-between are favorite interpretations, while the sorrows, humor, and earthiness of woodcutter, boatman, or innkeeper provide rich material for the Chinese comic actor. Solemn or harrowing themes are leavened by his laughter, and his skillful parody can carry his audience to the borders of a darker world. In all his parts he uses colloquial speech—he is the only actor on the traditional stage who does—but on occasion he also mimics the stylized vocal techniques of his fellow players. He makes great play with rhyming meters, and he is a superb exponent of the art of mime, which is not a separate kind of expression as it so often is in the West, but an integral element within the continuity of the acting form.

Wang Ch'uan-sung, the actor who played the comic role in the 1956 revival of *Fifteen Strings of Cash,* said in an interview: "A main principle in clowning is to seek the truth and avoid vulgarity. To make a deep impression on the audience, the actor should not behave as in real life but may even, if necessary, adopt some of the movements of animals or insects. A part of our training for K'unshan drama is called the 'play of the five noxious insects' and involves adaptations from certain movements of the toad, spider, snake, lizard, and centipede, movements utilized on the stage."

In the same interview, another famous comic actor, Hsiao Ch'ang-hua, emphasized the importance of artistic exaggeration in his roles. "By exaggeration I mean bringing out essential features emphatically through speech, action, and expression. This involves distilling and magnifying everyday life so that the audience sees the character more clearly than in actual life." Yet a third well known comic actor, Chou Chi-ho, said: "Humor is an art and we must rely on this art, not on meaningless antics, to make people laugh. . . . Good humor should not simply raise a smile at the time. The mere thought of a comic character should make one feel like laughing."[6]

The comments of these professionals reveal the essence of the comic actor's art, the elements which suggest an alchemical alloy of human failings and virtues. This constant fusion of essentially different experiences is the secret of the greatest comic performances; among these, the role of Lou the Rat remains outstanding in the annals of the Chinese theatre.

6. Unsigned interview in *Chinese Literature*, 1963, no. 4, pp. 104–13.

The Characters' Costumes

YU HU-LU

The robe traditionally worn in Yu Hu-lu's role is called a *ch'a-i,* which is used for tradesmen, servants, and so on.[7] It is made of a dark cobalt cotton and cut three-quarter length, with an open neck and a crossover fastening to the right. A broad black border decorates the neck opening and crossover, while the sleeves have narrow water sleeves. Beneath the robe, he wears wide, light-blue cotton trousers (*k'u-tzu*) tucked into thick, white cotton stockings. Chinese black cotton slippers with flat, white felt soles complete this stage dress (*see Fig. 11*). On his head the actor wears a *chan-mao,* a dark-blue woolen cap with a broad, up-turned brim and a wide, tasselled fringe on the crown. This hat is usually worn in comic and supernumerary roles. For makeup the actor wears a beard (*ssu-hsi jan*) which consists of two large wisps at either side of the face and a protruding moustache. Like all Chinese theatrical beards, it is constructed on a heavy wire frame supported on both ears and resting slightly above the top lip.

CH'IN KU-HSIN

Ch'in Ku-hsin wears a long robe called *lao-t'ou i,* used by elderly characters. It is of plain, tawny cloth with an open neck and a crossover opening to the right. The collar and crossover have a broad white border. The robe is split at either side and has

7. The costumes described in this section are those traditionally used, and may, on occasion, differ slightly from those shown in the photographs, which are of the 1956 Peking staging.

water sleeves. Beneath the robe the actor wears trousers tucked into white cotton stockings; black cotton slippers with flat, white felt soles complete the costume. Ch'in's beard, known as a *san-jan,* is made of white horsehair in three long sections: a broad central piece and a long, narrow strip on either side stretching from just below each ear. The beard completely covers the actor's mouth.

SU HSÜ-CHÜAN

Su Hsü-chüan wears a stage costume representing the dress of a young woman of humble circumstances, a maidservant, or as in this case, the daughter of a petty tradesman. Called *k'u-ao,* it consists of a short tunic with a high collar and neither water sleeves nor cuffs. The tunic has a slit in each side and fastens across the right breast and down the right side. It is worn with wide trousers and flat-soled, embroidered slippers. The tunic, together with the trousers, is made from plain colored satin, though blue cotton may also be used to emphasize her humble status (*see Fig. 3*). Over this is traditionally worn an apron (*wei-tsui*) which hangs to the waist; it is rounded at the top, being buttoned to the tunic below the collar and fastened at the back with tapes taken under the armpits (*see Fig. 4*). The apron is embroidered with a flower and butterfly pattern in bright colors on a black background, although other background colors, such as blue or green, may be used.

The coiffure is the standard *ta-fa* worn for female roles. Silver studs are placed on each of the symmetrical coils of hair framing the face, and four spear-shaped silver ornaments are fixed above these studs and around the form of the head. Above these, another row of small silver decorations is placed diagonally from left to right. The large chignon is surrounded by a circlet of the same ornaments, and two large silver pins are placed upright in the chignon, one above the other. A cluster of artificial flowers is fixed to each side of the coiffure above the ears, and two long braids of hair hang down from the main coiffure over each shoulder at the front to reach below the waist. In Scene 4, the execution scene before K'uang Chung, all the decorations have been removed from Su Hsü-chüan's coiffure, leaving only the plain black

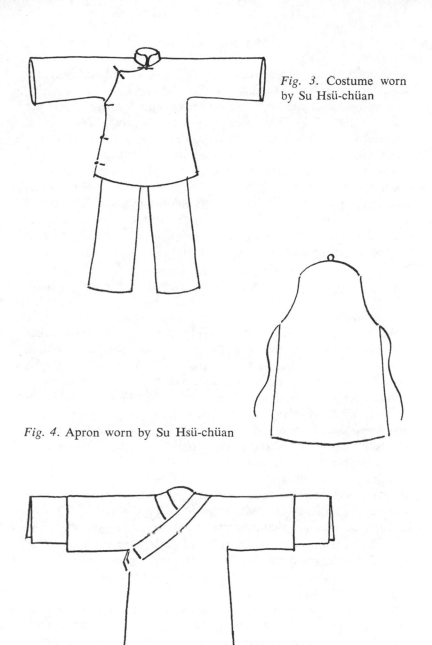

Fig. 3. Costume worn
by Su Hsü-chüan

Fig. 4. Apron worn by Su Hsü-chüan

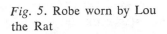

Fig. 5. Robe worn by Lou
the Rat

foundation hairdo, from which a long, thick strand has been released to hang down over the left shoulder.

For the facial makeup, the eyebrows and the eye shape are boldly pencilled in, and both eyes are elongated. The face is covered with a heavy white base, obliterating the lips. Rouge is applied over this so that a deep red tone covers the eyelids and the area beneath the eyes, and then is graded off to more subdued tones on the cheeks and side of the nose. The bridge of the nose, forehead, upper lip, and chin are left entirely in white. The mouth is then redefined with lipstick, making it smaller than the natural form. This style of makeup is basic to most of the younger women's roles on the traditional Chinese stage.

LOU THE RAT

Lou the Rat wears a black cotton, three-quarter-length robe (*ch'ing p'ao*) which has short water sleeves and a slit on either side of the garment (*see Fig. 5*). It has an open neck with a crossover fastening from left to right, the left portion of the robe being fastened under the right armpit with tapes. The neckband is outlined with two bands of white piping about three inches apart. A white silk stock (*hu-ling*) is worn crossover style and is visible about two inches above the collar line. The robe is lined with pale blue silk. It is worn by characters of lower rank. Beneath the robe are wide black cotton trousers tucked into thick, stiff, cotton stockings worn calf height. The actor wears plain black cotton, flat-soled slippers (*Fig. 11*). Lou the Rat's hat, known as a *hei lo-mao,* is made of black satin and could be described as a kind of hexagonal tam-o'-shanter crowned by a small pompon (*Fig. 12*). This hat is much smaller than a similar style worn by actors who play swordsmen and fighters; it fits more closely to the head and is worn by servants and characters of lower rank.

Lou's facial makeup is universal for the clown on the Chinese stage: a white patch covering the nose and cheek area with various black markings superimposed. In this case, the makeup is confined largely to the nose, and the area is carried slightly more over to the left cheek than to the right. A circular, white-bordered black spot is painted on each temple; there is the suggestion of a moustache on the upper lip, a white marking beneath the lower lip, and a curved white line like a scar around the form of the left cheek. The plates will give an idea of this makeup in use.

HSIUNG YU-LAN

Hsiung Yu-lan wears a costume symbolizing a young merchant. His thigh-length robe, called *su-juan hsüeh-tzu,* is of light-blue cloth and is knotted around the waist with a sash that hangs down in front to just below the hem of the robe (*see Fig. 6*). The robe has an open neck with a crossover collar worn tied under the right armpit with tapes. The collar has a broad, dark-blue outer facing about three inches wide; a white silk stock is worn crossover style beneath the collar. The robe has short water sleeves. He wears black trousers, white stockings, and black slippers in the same style as those worn by Lou the Rat. His hat is like Yu Hu-lu's.

In Scene 3, when Hsiung is dragged back on stage after being punished in an attempt to extort a confession from him, his hat has been removed. A long plume of black horsehair (*shuai-fa*), fixed to a short vertical support and hanging down from the crown of his head, has been substituted. The small wooden base of the plume is fixed with tapes to a small metal support (*ta-tsan*), which in turn is fitted beneath the skullcap (*wang-tzu*) that forms the basis of the actor's coiffure. The plume is always worn to symbolize a prisoner or a man in distress; the actor manipulates it with vigorous head movements to emphasize emotional climaxes on the stage.

KUO YÜ-CHIH

The district magistrate wears a long robe known as a *kuan-i* which is inspired by the official robes worn in the old imperial civil service of China (*see Fig. 9*). These robes followed strict usage in style, cut, color, symbolism, and insignia. Theatrical considerations have dictated the stage versions, and they should not be considered historical models, as they frequently are by Chinese film studios; nevertheless, the stage adaptation of Ming official costume reflects more accurately the form of costumes that were actually used than do many stage costumes. (Water sleeves, of

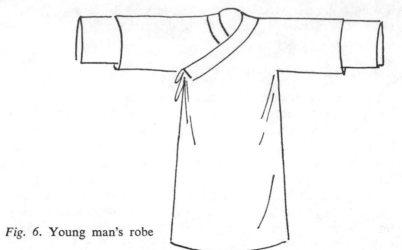

Fig. 6. Young man's robe

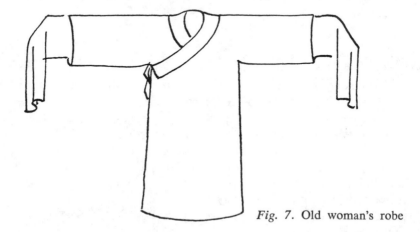

Fig. 7. Old woman's robe

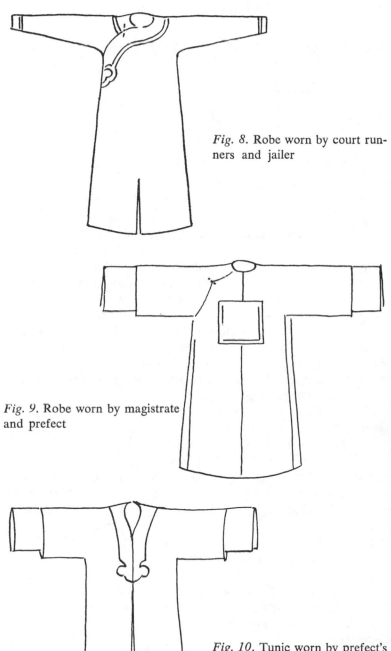

Fig. 8. Robe worn by court runners and jailer

Fig. 9. Robe worn by magistrate
and prefect

Fig. 10. Tunic worn by prefect's
assistant in peddler's disguise

Fig. 11. Left, slippers worn by Yu Hu-lu and Lou the Rat; *center,* high, platform-soled boots worn by magistrate, prefect, and governor; *right,* ankle-length boots worn by executioners and court runners.

course, are a purely theatrical device and were never used by officials in real life.)

There were eight principal ranks of officials in the old provincial civil service, ranging from Governor General to Assistant District Magistrate. Each rank was distinguished by variations in the colors and insignia of its official dress. On the Peking stage, officials between the First and Fourth Ranks wear a crimson robe (*hung kuan-i*); if they are elderly the robe is purple (*tzu kuan-i*), and this is the style worn by Kuo Yü-chih. It is a voluminous garment with wide sleeves and generous water sleeves. It has a low-cut, circular neck opening, beneath which is worn a white stock in crossover style. The robe is slit to the thigh on either side and has a crossover fastening at the right side. A stiff, hoop-like girdle (*yü-tai*) is worn around the waist; it far exceeds the circumference of the actor's form and is attached through loops on the sides of the robe. On the front of the robe, across the chest of the actor, is a twelve-inch-square, embroidered panel called *p'u-tzu,* which has a symbolic crane, cloud, and sun motif enclosed within a deep border. This represents a rank insignia. The hat worn by the magistrate, the *sha-mao,* is made of stiff black felt with a double, semicircular crown (*Fig. 12*). From the rear at either side protrude two fins, or *ch'ih,* which are so made as to quiver slightly with the actor's head movements. In this case the fins are shaped somewhat like the blade of an oar with a rounded end. The magistrate wears high, platform-soled boots of soft, black satin known as *kuan-hsüeh* (*Fig. 11*). Their wedge-shaped soles are painted white.

Fig. 12. Left, hats worn by magistrate, prefect, and governor; *center,* headdress worn by the governor's guards; *top right,* hat worn by Lou the Rat; *bottom right,* hat worn by K'uang Chung in fortune-teller's disguise.

Kuo Yü-chih's beard, made of gray horsehair and completely covering his mouth, is the same type of beard as that worn by Ch'in Ku-hsin.

K'UANG CHUNG

The prefect wears three costumes during the play. His official costume, worn in Scenes 4, 6, and 8, is like that of Kuo Yü-chih, the district magistrate, except that K'uang's robe is crimson. K'uang is a younger man than the magistrate, and his beard is therefore black instead of white.

For his audience with the governor in Scene 5, K'uang has changed from his official crimson robe to one of similar cut and style, but made of plain black satin. In Scene 7 he is disguised as a fortune-teller. Disguise on the traditional Chinese stage is a question of symbolism rather than any attempt at real concealment. A character is always perfectly obvious as the same character; the costume or accessories are changed only enough to suggest the disguise. K'uang wears a plain, long black satin robe (*su-juan hsüeh-tzu*) that resembles Hsiung Yu-lan's in style, with a crossover collar fastening faced in white and with long water sleeves. He wears high, white-soled black satin boots and a hat known as a *fang-chin (see Fig. 12)*. He has a full, black beard and a red circular spot painted on the center of his brow between the eyebrows. In his right hand he has a large folding fan; in his left he carries a small, rectangular wooden tablet inscribed with the Chinese characters (*kuan mei ts'e tzu*) for a Taoist fortune-teller.

CHOU CH'EN

The governor has a white beard and wears an ocher costume and headdress. His robe, called a *mang,* is based on a style once worn by high officials. It is a voluminous garment covering the feet and has very wide sleeves with water sleeves attached. It is slit at either side and has a low-cut, circular neck opening, beneath which is worn a white silk stock. The robe hangs in heavy folds, fastens to the right, and is elaborately patterned with an intricately woven dragon design and a deep border with wave and key motifs. His double-crowned hat is similar to the magistrate's, the two protruding fins being about two inches wide and eighteen inches long. A jade girdle and high-soled boots like those worn by the magistrate and prefect complete the governor's costume.

NEIGHBORS A, B, C, AND D

The two elderly women characters both wear plain, long skirts, one white and the other dark blue. The elderly woman dressed in the white skirt wears a robe called *nü lao-t'ou i* over the skirt (*Fig. 7*). The robe is cut about nine inches above the hem of the skirt and has the open neck, crossover collar, and long water sleeves characteristic of this class of stage garment, of which there are several variations. In this case, the robe is a light umber with a broad, black collar facing. A white stock is worn crossover style to show above the collar. The second elderly woman wears a plain, knee-length robe similar to the one just described, the length being the differing factor. Over this robe is worn a plain-colored, knee-length, sleeveless robe (*su nü pei-hsin*) that is slit at either side and has a black collarband. Both women wear a gray, semicircular skullcap (*wang-tzu*) made of horsehair and bound with silk; it opens at the back with two tapes to fasten it to the head. A broad bandeau of colored silk is bound around the skullcap, practically covering the ears and wound low on the forehead just above the eyebrows.

The young man neighbor wears the same kind of costume as Hsiung Yu-lan, except that his robe is dark blue and the collar of the robe is white. The young woman neighbor is dressed in the same fashion as Su Hsü-chüan and represents a girl of the same class. Her tunic and trousers are made of blue cotton, as against the pale blue satin of Su Hsü-chüan's garments.

COURT RUNNERS

Each of the runners wears an ankle-length, black cotton robe (*tsao-li i*) slit at the sides and at the center front and rear (*see Fig. 8*). It has long sleeves which narrow at the cuff and fit closely around the wrist; the broad white cuff is decorated with a single narrow blue stripe. The neck is open with a crossover fastening and a broad blue collarband that is continued around the fastening and has thin white piping; a white stock is worn crossover style in the neckline. The robe is bound around the waist by a stiff orange sash (*luan-tai*) with long, tasselled ends hanging nearly to the ankles at the front. The wide, ankle-length, crimson trousers worn beneath the robe are tucked into ankle-length, flat-soled, black satin boots called *pao-ti hsüeh* (*see Fig. 11*). The hat, a recent addition to the stage wardrobe, can best be studied in Plate 6. Great attention was paid to the supernumeraries of the traditional stage during the early fifties, and various new patterns were devised to make them a little more conspicuous.

The disguise that one of the runners wears in Scene 7 is the same kind of costume as that worn by Yu Hu-lu, with one addition: a pleated white skirt tied around the waist and hanging below the knees. This costume represents someone of the rank of shopkeeper or waiter.

COURT ATTENDANTS

Two different styles of dress are used for the court attendants, one, for the attendants in the Wuhsi District Court, and the other, for the attendants in the Soochow prefectural court. The attendants in the district court wear the costume previously described for the court runners. Each attendant in the prefectural court wears a simple, loose, black cotton robe (*ch'ing-p'ao*). It covers the feet and has long, wide sleeves that hide the hands completely when the arms are extended by the sides. The robe sometimes has water sleeves, but in this case they are omitted. The attendants wear soft woolen, crimson, conical caps with wide, upturned brims.

EXECUTIONERS

The executioners wear costumes called *k'uei tzu shou-i* in crimson with black facings. The wide crimson trousers are tucked into black satin, ankle-length, flat-soled boots (*Fig. 11*). Their ornate headdress is a kind of coronet, ornamented with a single six-foot-long pheasant plume worn to the right by two of the executioners and to the left by the other two. It is technically known as a *k'uei*, or helmet, and in this case is a new modification of a traditional style worn by military officials. Each executioner carries a scimitar (*tao*). Plate 7 shows the executioners in costume.

JAILER

The jailer wears a woolen cap like Yu Hu-lu's, except that it is white. His robe is of the same style and colors as the robe worn by the court runners (*Fig. 8*); and it, too, has an orange sash around the waist. His black trousers are tucked into calf-length, thick, white cotton stockings, over which he wears plain, black, flat-soled shoes. He wears a white beard like the one worn by Yu Hu-lu.

ASSISTANT TO K'UANG CHUNG

The robe of the prefect's assistant is similar to the robes worn by the attendants in the prefectural court, except that it is made of black satin, has water sleeves, and is fastened around the waist with a thin girdle. The assistant wears a wig representing a bobbed coiffure with a fringe cut low on the forehead. Around this is a narrow bandeau with a looped bow at either side of the head; a long silk tassel nearly reaching the shoulders is suspended from each bow. This headdress traditionally symbolizes a boy or youth, although the use of the wig is a new feature and may follow film usage. In the 1956 Peking production this supernumerary role was played by an actress.

When the assistant appears in disguise as a peddler in Scene 7, his headdress is the same, but his robe has been replaced with a costume called an *erh-i,* which consists of a blue tunic and wide trousers. The tunic has short water sleeves and black collar facings (*see Fig. 10*). A blue sash is worn around the waist. He carries a pole of his own height in his left hand; the pole has a crosspiece from which colored silk threads and tassels hang. In his right hand he carries a small, drum-shaped rattle used by hawkers to notify possible customers of their approach.

NIGHT DUTY OFFICER

The actor in this role wears a military official's costume (*k'ai-ch'ang*) having water sleeves and patterned with heraldic lions and peonies in blue, gold, and white. He has a black mustachio (*pa-tzu*) whose two bristling ends protrude forward.

CAPTAIN OF THE GUARD AND GUARDS

The captain of the guard wears a riding jacket (*tuan lung ma-kua*) with a waist-length opening down the front and a circular neck opening. It has wide, wrist-length sleeves bordered in a broad wave pattern; the same border also decorates the hem of the garment. There is a large dragon roundel on each sleeve and on the front and back of the jacket. The jacket is worn over an ankle-length robe (*lung chien-i*) slit at the front and rear, with close-fitting, tight cuffed sleeves and an open neck with a crossover fastening. A stiff, knotted sash is worn around the waist. The whole costume is in blue, silver, and black. A gold hat with a circular, upturned brim and a bucket-shaped crown, from which hangs a gold tassel, and the official, high-soled boots (*kuan-hsüeh*) are worn with this costume. The captain carries a sword at his left.

Each of the guards wears a short, crimson riding jacket (*ma-kua*) with an embroidered roundel on the front and back. A white silk stock is visible above the collarless neck opening, and a broad orange sash like that worn by the court runners hangs down at the front beneath the jacket. The guards wear wide trousers and flat-soled boots similar to those described for the court runners. The hat is a version of a style called *wu-sheng chin* (*see Fig. 12*). Beneath the hat is a long strand of black hair, bound beneath the skullcap and hanging to waist height at either side of the face. Each guard carries a Chinese lantern suspended from a short stick held in the right hand and supported by the left.

HEADMAN

The headman wears a blue robe called *su chien-i,* which is very similar in style to the robe described for the court runners, and is bound around the waist by a similar orange sash. The headman wears a semi-stiff hat which could best be described as boat-shaped. It has a broad, upturned brim bordered in blue, the hat itself being of black felt. Plate 8, in which the headman stands just to the left of K'uang Chung, shows this costume.

Fifteen Strings of Cash

Scene 1: The Evil Deed of Lou the Rat

The main stage is curtained off, leaving a performing area front stage.

Yu Hu-lu enters left of the audience. He is drunk and staggers in his steps, which nevertheless are performed with the formalized patterns of movement common to traditional acting. The foot movement used is known as yun-pu and is carried out by placing the left foot apart, dragging it up obliquely to the right foot three times in succession, and then repeating the sequence with the right foot in the other direction. This gait can be alternated with a similar pattern of steps in which one foot is crossed over the other each time the body sways drunkenly but rhythmically.

Over his left shoulder Yu Hu-lu carries the fifteen strings of cash, copper coins pierced through their centers and threaded on strings in the old Chinese fashion. He heaves the coins with a jingle as he drunkenly addresses the audience:

YU HU-LU: A-ah! What a weight!
  (*He begins to sing in the Liu Yao Ling modal pattern.*)
  The more wine I drink, the better I'll be;
  The more money I spend, the less I'll keep.
  I was sad in heart so long without trade.
  To secure a loan, I've run around everywhere.
  (*He relapses into monologue before the audience.*)
  Consider me, Yu Hu-lu. Since I closed down my pork shop, I've had to rely on pawning and borrowing to keep going. Every day I've been distracted with the thought of it. My late wife's sister lives at Kaoch'iao. She's a faithful, affec-

tionate soul, and today she invited me to drink a couple of
jugs of wine and lent me these fifteen strings of cash to go
into business again. I'm feeling very happy indeed.
(*He begins singing again.*)
Sister's heart is full of true kindness;
Those who help the poor and needy are rare in this world.
I left her house as dusk fell.
The watch is on his round already and my journey's done.
(*He relapses into monologue again.*)
Before, when I bought a pig, I relied entirely on my old
friend Ch'in to help me. I'm going to buy a pig tomorrow, so
now I'll just go and see if he'll help. (*Crosses the stage to
stand left of the audience.*) This is his door. (*Shouting.*)
Hey, Ch'in, old friend, are you home? Ch'in!

CH'IN KU-HSIN (*behind the curtain*): Who's that outside?

YU HU-LU (*feigning a girlish voice*): It's me.
(*He makes an ugly face. Ch'in Ku-hsin comes on.*)

CH'IN KU-HSIN: So it's friend Yu! It's too late to play jokes like
this. What do you want?

YU HU-LU: Look at this, my old friend. (*He holds up the cash.*)

CH'IN KU-HSIN (*his face expressing astonishment*): Where did all
that money come from?

YU HU-LU (*heaving the cash to the floor with a jangle and then
straightening himself to speak*): Picked it up on the street!

CH'IN KU-HSIN: You're joking again! (*He is standing to the right
of Yu, right arm behind his back and left hand raised to chest
height as he speaks.*)

YU HU-LU (*leans backward, laughing uproariously, and gesticulates
with his right hand*): I'll deceive you no more. My sister-in-
law at Kaoch'iao lent me these fifteen strings of cash to go
into business again. (*He stoops to pick up the cash and slings
them over his left shoulder again.*)

CH'IN KU-HSIN (*emphasizing his words with his right hand*): Good,
good! Now you've got some capital, you can open up your
shop again with no more financial worries. It'll be to my ad-
vantage too; my oil and wine sales will go up. If you like,
tomorrow we'll go together and buy a pig.

YU HU-LU: Thanks very much, old friend.

CH'IN KU-HSIN: But I'm afraid you're so drunk you'll forget. I'll
    come and call for you.
YU HU-LU (*stands swaying slightly and answers in a convivial
    tone*): Thanks very much indeed!
CH'IN KU-HSIN: See you tomorrow. (*He goes off stage to the left.*[8])
YU HU-LU (*walking unsteadily to front stage center*): Leaving
    Ch'in's oil and salt store, I arrive at my own pork shop. (*He
    faces the curtain and calls out loudly while miming knocking
    at the door, coordinating voice and gesture.*) Open the door!
    Open the door! Open the door!
    (*The curtain is opened to show the interior of Yu Hu-lu's
    pork shop, the second acting area. The use of curtains in this
    way has become customary since 1949, allowing for greater
    use of stage settings and the disappearance from view of the
    old stage assistant. The stage is carpeted, as always in the
    Chinese theatre. Against the curtain backdrop two rectangu-
    lar panels nine feet high are placed to represent the walls of
    the shop. The back one, flush with the rear curtain, is painted
    to represent plaster and brick and has a sign suspended in
    the top right-hand corner. On the sign are painted Chinese
    characters which read "Yu's Butcher Shop." At the front of
    this panel and to the left, almost at center stage, is Yu Hu-lu's
    bed. This is a rectangular construction, a low dais painted to
    represent wooden planking, with a bamboo pole at each
    corner and crosspieces supporting an embroidered curtain
    looped back in front of the bed. The second wall of the shop,
    placed to make a wide angle with the first, to the right of
    the stage from the audience, is painted to represent wooden
    planking, against which two meat hooks hang from a wooden
    support. In front of this wall stands a four-legged butcher's
    wooden chopping block, on which a large axe is placed. This*

---

8. The normal entry (*shang ch'ang*) is to the left of the audience and the
normal exit (*hsia ch'ang*) to the right. The actor both enters and exits
through the first to indicate a return to the original place of departure.
To indicate a summons from someone already on stage, the actor both
enters and exits through the second. If characters enter from both directions, this represents a chance meeting. If exits are made through both
points again, it represents going in different directions.

set is a concession to the naturalism that increasingly dom-
inates the Chinese Communist stage. In the old days a simple,
small wooden table with bamboo poles and curtains would
have sufficed for the bed and that would have been all. In
the context of the highly formalized mime and movement of
traditional acting, this preoccupation with set details serves
little dramatic function except to emphasize the obvious.

On hearing her father's voice, Su Hsü-chüan appears to the
left of the stage to the audience. She calls out on making her
entry.)

SU HSÜ-CHÜAN: I'm coming.

(She then crosses the stage to open the door, a traditional
mime described in the previous play. As his daughter mimes
opening the door, Yu Hu-lu stands parallel to it, facing the
left side of the stage to the audience, as though listening to
the bolts being shot. After opening the door, Su Hsü-chüan
leans forward, head and shoulders tilted to the right, and
placing her hands beneath her father's right arm, is about
to help him indoors.)

Oh, there you are, Father.

YU HU-LU: Here I am.

SU HSÜ-CHÜAN (*looking at the strings of cash on his shoulder*):
Wherever did you get so much money?

YU HU-LU (*his voice heavy with wine*): Guess where I got it!

SU HSÜ-CHÜAN: Did you borrow it?

YU HU-LU: Where is there anybody kind enough to lend me so
much?

SU HSÜ-CHÜAN: Then were did you get it?

(Yu Hu-lu raises his right arm to address her, and as he
speaks, punctuates his words with his first and middle fingers
together and extended, the thumb, fourth finger, and little
finger touching at the tips. His voice, still thick with wine, is
bantering in tone.)

YU HU-LU: Ai, it's no good hiding it from you; it's come to this
now. When I went out this morning, I happened to meet
old mother Chiang, the go-between. She told me Wang Yuan-
wai's daughter is going to be married and is short of a slave
girl in her dowry. So I sold you to her for fifteen strings of
cash.

(*Su Hsü-chüan starts back in alarm at hearing her father's words. Her right arm, bent at the elbow, is placed against her right breast, hand curved back, fingers crooked. The left arm is thrust forward at a slightly lower level, though with the elbow still half bent. The middle finger and thumb are placed together in each hand. The left shoulder is raised a little higher than the right and her head tilted slightly downwards. She holds herself at a little distance from her father and steps back two paces at his final words.*)

SU HSÜ-CHÜAN: Are you really telling the truth?

YU HU-LU (*wagging his fingers at her*): They want you to go early tomorrow morning. You'd better get your things together quickly and be ready.

(*Su Hsü-chüan gives a loud wail of grief, the traditional high crescendo of sound that drops away in a drawn-out cadence, as she quickly makes her exit to the right of the stage to the audience.*)

SU HSÜ-CHÜAN: Aiya! Oh, Mother!

YU HU-LU (*overcome with drunken laughter and addressing the audience*): What a joke! She really believes it. We'll tease her for tonight and tell her the truth tomorrow morning.

(*He turns away as though pondering for a moment, facing left stage from the audience. His right leg is forward and slightly bent; his left hand is raised to caress his beard. His right arm, elbow bent, is raised a little above face level; the water sleeve hangs down. In this position, he turns around as though peering into the lamplight and goes towards the bed.*) I'll put the money safely away, and then I shall sleep well. (*He puts the strings of cash beneath the hard, round pillow at the head of the bed, but the cash is only half hidden and hangs down over the edge of the bed, nearly touching the floor. He then gets onto the bed and composes himself for sleep beneath the curtains, his head on the pillow, his arms folded over his chest, and his left leg crossed over the knee of his bent right leg. This is a typical sleeping posture on the traditional Chinese stage, particularly when a scene of action or violence is to follow.*

Su Hsü-chüan enters left of the stage to the audience. She is in distress and begins to sing in the Shang P'o Yang modal pattern. As she sings, she walks slowly, pausing for each line, with one leg slightly bent and poised on the toes placed just behind the heel of the forward foot, which is squarely on the floor. She emphasizes her lines with her raised hands, first the right hand, then the left. The fingers are delicately curved in the traditional position for female roles: the thumb and middle finger are held together in a curve, the index finger is extended, the fourth finger is crooked slightly above the center of the middle finger, and the little finger is curved above the center of the fourth finger.)

SU HSÜ-CHÜAN (*sings*):

My heart is sad, my tears drop down.
I am like a frail boat on the boundless ocean,
Tossed by the breakers and unable to reach the peaceful
    shore.
I will plead with him, for my dead mother's sake,
To reconsider selling the body of his lonely child,
Like goods for cash.

(She has approached the bed at this point and stands looking down on the sleeping man. Her right arm is bent at a right angle across her waist, the hand raised towards the left arm, which is extended at waist height. Her head is slightly inclined, and her body faces towards the right of the stage to the audience. She cries out:)

Father, Father!

(But Yu Hu-lu is fast asleep and Su Hsü-chüan begins to sing again.)

I am not his own child,
So he sold me with a smile
Just as though I were a stranger.
How can I make him take pity on me?
I fear it is difficult to persuade him
To change his mind.
It's worse than boiling in oil.
I implore the heavens ten million times.
It's as though my heart were pierced with arrows.
I call upon my mother, call until my lips are dry!

(As she sings, her steps have taken her towards the butcher's block, on which lies the axe. The thought enters her mind to die. She stands posing for a moment. Her body is inclined

*towards the block; her head is turned away over her left
shoulder. Her right arm is across her body with her left hand
resting lightly on her right forearm above the wrist. The third
and middle fingers only lightly touch the sleeve, while the
index and little fingers are delicately poised. She picks up
the axe, holding it at chest height and away from the body,
and turns towards the audience. The left arm still supports
the right arm. The index finger of the right hand is extended
behind the blade of the axe; the remaining fingers grasp the
handle. Su Hsü-chüan stares fixedly at the axe, then puts it
down on the block again as she changes her mind.)*
But wait! I remember my aunt at Kaoch'iao once telling me
that if I was ever in difficulty to go to her. Things have
reached such a dreadful pass, the best plan would be to do
that first.
(Sings in the Ma Shang Shui Hung Ling modal pattern:)
If only my aunt can save me from all this trouble!
I'll take this opportunity while he is in drunken sleep
To go to my relative without delay.
*(She moves to center front stage, mimes opening the shop
door but does not close it, steps hastily through, pauses, then
runs off stage to the right of the audience.)*

*(The stage is now set for the entry of the central character,
Lou the Rat. From now on his presence and his deeds will
dominate the course of the play. He is the villain, but more
than that, he is the fulcrum for the theatricality of this piece,
and the mood and rhythm generated by his performance carry
the audience along from this point.*

*Lou the Rat comes on yawning, his bent arms stretched to
head height, his fists clenched. He goes to front center stage
and turns to address the audience. His weight is on his right
foot; his left knee is slightly bent with the left heel lifted from
the floor a little. His right arm is placed across his waist to
the left and supports the elbow of his raised left arm, as he
strokes his chin thoughtfully. He recites a couplet which
rhymes in Chinese.)*
LOU THE RAT:
I've lost every penny I possess at gambling.
I must find another dupe.

(He faces the audience squarely, eyes wide, and speaks in tones of confidential earnestness adopted by the Clown. His left foot is squarely forward, knee bent, and his right foot is placed obliquely to the rear, knee bent. He indicates his own person with his right hand at chest height. His raised left arm, elbow bent, hand open, and palm upwards, is directed towards the audience. He recites in colloquial speech:)

Consider me, Lou the Rat. I've neither goods nor land and rely solely on gambling for a living. Never mind about the Four Classes of Society, the Three Doctrines, and the Nine Schools of Philosophy.[9] I'm only interested in a man if he has money. If I can swindle, I swindle; if I'm able to steal, then it's convenient to steal. You may think I've a bad reputation, but I've many sworn brothers at the gambling tables and friends in the Yamen;[10] all the people of this neighborhood have to treat me with proper respect. Yesterday I cheated a fellow out of a little money, but I had horrible luck and lost the lot at the tables. Even though my dice were loaded, they were all seasoned hands in the gambling rooms this evening, and I wasn't able to turn over even a little cash for myself. I want to find the God of Wealth quickly and get his blessing!

(He stops and looks furtively this way and that. He sees the open door of the butcher's shop, indicated entirely by his expression and gesture, of course, and turns towards the audience again, a smile on his face. He leans forward confidentially from the waist, his feet in the position previously described. His arms are raised at waist height, the palms of his open hands down; the left hand, slightly higher than the right, punctuates his words to the audience.)

Eh, why is the door of Yu Hu-lu's house open and the lamp

---

9. "Four Classes of Society." (*Ssu Min*) is a reference to the fact that Chinese society was formerly classified in four main groups—scholar, farmer, artisan, and merchant. The Three Doctrines (*San Chiao*) were Confucianism, Buddhism, and Taoism; and the Nine Schools of Philosophy, or Literature (*Chiu Liu*) were Confucian, Taoist, Divination, Law, Logic, Mo-tzu, Politics, Agriculture, and Miscellaneous.

10. The official and private residence of any government official entitled to a seal of Imperial authority.

not yet out? It looks as though they've killed a pig again. Wait. I'll get a few catties of pork on credit and eat a good meal before I do anything else.

(*He mimes crossing the threshold and stands with his back to the audience. He calls out the names of the butcher and his daughter.*)

Yu, my friend! Miss!

(*There is no reply. He confides in the audience again. He stands obliquely facing to the right of the audience; his right hand holds the bottom of his left sleeve, and his left hand is raised, fingers clenched and thumb outstretched, as he indicates the sleeping pork butcher behind. His body is inclined towards the right, and he stands squarely on his right foot, left knee bent, left heel raised.*)

Why he's fast asleep. It looks as though he got very drunk and forgot to put out the light and close the door. (*Turning his head.*) Ah! There's a meat chopper on the table. I might as well creep over and get it to pawn for a few cash.

(*He walks stealthily over, seizes the meat chopper, and turns to face the bed. His body is bent double, right foot forward, right hand grasping the chopper at the left side of his waist, the fingers of the left hand outstretched, and his bent left arm slightly raised above the right, as he exclaims:*)

Aiya! I see a lot of money underneath his pillow. Well, this is unexpected!

(*He puts the chopper back on the table and recites the following lines.*)

My lucky star is shining high
To match my smiles.

(*He pauses and looks around fearfully.*)

And yet my mind's confused:
I tremble.[11]

(*He addresses the audience.*)

---

11. In the Chinese original, this is a three-line stanza with a syllabic pattern of four, four, four and a rhyming ending to each line:

ts'ai hsing kao chao
mei k'ai yen hsiao
hsin huang nei t'iao.

Just now I was worried for lack of capital, but now that I
have some, I need no longer be melancholy.
(*He is standing with his left foot bent, heel lifted, as he
speaks. He raises both arms, and with a circular movement
across the waist, points towards the bed and the sleeping
man. The index and middle fingers, placed together, are used
for the pointing gesture. He addresses the audience again.*)
I'll go to the gaming house and play for high stakes.
(*Recites.*)
I'll go to the wine shop to drink my fill,
Then to the gay quarters for some fun.[12]
(*He pauses as if the thought of future possibilities had re-
stored his momentary fears. Then he turns right of the stage
to the audience, arms held at waist height and knees lifted
high with exaggerated steps as he mimes creeping silently
towards the bed, which he approaches by swinging around
in a small arc from his starting position—i.e., he moves to
the right of stage from the audience, turns with his back
towards them, and then moves towards the bed. He pauses
at a distance of about three feet, then suddenly goes down on
his hands and knees, and begins to tug gently on the strings
of cash. He pulls the strings in jerks from the bottom near
the floor. As he pulls, the sleeping butcher stirs, and Lou
the Rat falls flat on his face in alarm. He raises his head
gingerly. Since all seems well, he kneels and begins pulling
the cash again. Finally he pries them loose, and as he does,
Yu Hu-lu sits up, leaning on his left elbow and gazing at the
thief. Lou the Rat, still sitting on his haunches, his left leg
slightly bent and heel lifted, holds the filched cash in both
hands. His right hand is forward from the left and nearest
to the end string of cash trailing on the floor.*)
YU HU-LU (*coming to himself suddenly*): Who is it? Confound it,
    it's a thief! (*He tumbles from the bed and grasps hold of
    Lou the Rat, who has jumped to his feet.*) So it's you! Lou
    the Rat! You haven't yet paid me what you already owe me
    for pork, and still you want to steal from me!

---

12. The last two lines make a rhyming couplet with a syllabic pattern
of seven, seven:

> ch'u tao chiu-kuan ch'ih ko pao
> tsai tao chi-yuan tsou i tsao.

(He tries to regain the cash, which Lou the Rat has slung over his left shoulder. The two struggle in a kind of tug-of-war in front of the bed and finish with Yu Hu-lu hanging onto one end of the strings of cash and Lou the Rat bent double at the other end, his back towards the chopping block, in the direction of which he is straining. Yu Hu-lu, still upright, refuses to let go, but as they near the block, Lou the Rat stretches out and seizes the chopper. The cash have dropped to the floor. The two men face each other. Yu Hu-lu has his fists clenched in a sparring attitude, left fist foremost. Lou the Rat is leaning over to one side, his left fist clenched, palm uppermost, his elbow drawn in to his waist. His right hand grasps the chopper at waist height in front of him. With a quick jab he aims the weapon at Yu Hu-lu's throat, and the pork butcher falls flat on the floor parallel to the bed, arms by his side, legs stretched out, toes turned up, and his face towards the ceiling. His feet are towards the left of the stage to the audience. Lou the Rat stands posed above his victim between Yu Hu-lu and the bed, his right leg near his victim's left leg, his left foot placed well back in an oblique stance to the forward foot. He leans forward on his right foot; his right arm is still forward holding the chopper, his left arm drawn back with clenched fist. He remains in this position a few seconds before finally straightening up again after seeing his adversary is indeed dead.)

LOU THE RAT: Yu Hu-lu! Yu Hu-lu! You won't criticize my sleight of hand again. If I hadn't killed you, you'd have run outside telling everybody about me, wouldn't you? I know,

(He picks up the fallen cash and slings it over his left shoulder, grasping it with his right hand. He faces the audience and recites.)

If I'd not done it,
There would have been no rest afterwards.
From the broken pot
No more oil[13] will flow.
Take the strings of cash
And quickly, quickly slip away!

---

13. This is a pun in the original, the pork butcher's name, "Yu," having the same Chinese character as that used for "oil."

(He has crept towards the door of the shop, front center stage, and is about to step outside when he hears the sound of the night watchman.[14] *Starting back in alarm, he retreats into the shop, and with cupped hands, mimes blowing out a lamp. Then he darts behind the bed, placing the cash on the bed as he does so, and appears half hidden between the bed and the wall in an attitude of suspense. After the watch has passed, he picks up the cash. As he hurriedly emerges, half of one of the strings of cash falls behind the bed; he scrambles for it in vain and hastens to the door. A dice box falls unnoticed from his sleeve as he moves away and rolls beneath the bed. At the door he furtively sticks his head out and looks from side to side to reassure himself no one is around. Then he steps quickly over the threshold and runs off stage to the right of the audience, the cash over his left shoulder.)*

(There is a pause, and then old Ch'in Ku-hsin enters left of the audience. Although there is no curtain or any break in the continuity of action, the lights, which had been lowered in the previous scene, are full on again to indicate that it is now the next morning. As he walks to front center stage, Ch'in Ku-hsin recites a couplet in the style known as kan-pan, in which the rhythm of the lines is given percussive emphasis with the beats of a hardwood clapper used by the leader of the orchestra.)

CH'IN KU-HSIN:

Kinsman helps kinsman;
Neighbor helps neighbor;
The rich help the rich;
And the poor help the poor.
(He has now arrived front center stage and starts in surprise at finding the door open.)
What, the front door open? He must be up already! *(He*

---

14. In China there used to be five night watches of two hours each from 7 P.M. to 5 A.M., and these were beaten out on a large drum placed in a special tower overlooking the city. The watchman made five rounds in each watch, and he carried a small wooden block on which to beat out the number of hours relevant to each watch with a small wooden stick. It is this sound that startles Lou the Rat.

enters, miming crossing the threshold, and once inside, calls out.) Yu Hu-lu! Yu Hu-lu!

(*There is no reply, and as he moves forward, he trips against the outstretched legs of the dead man. He starts back. He stands straddled across the feet of the corpse, bending over to look down at it. Old Ch'in's left foot is supported on the heel turned obliquely from the right foot; his arms are lifted at waist height, and he gestures with the right hand, middle finger and index finger placed together, in indicating the corpse.*)

Ah, what's this I've tripped over on the floor? So it's my old friend Yu. Hey, Yu, get up! Why do you want to sleep on the floor when you have such a fine bed? (*He leans over to prod Yu and then straightens up in alarm.*) O-oh! His body's covered with blood. He's been murdered! (*He calls to Yu's daughter.*)

Miss! Miss!

(*There is no reply.*)

She's not to be found either!

(*He goes hastily to the door, and stepping over the threshold, begins to call out at the top of his voice.*)

Hey, you neighbors! Hey, you neighbors! Come quickly; something awful's happened!

(*Neighbors A, B, C, and D—two elderly women, a young man, and a young woman—quickly enter the stage from front left and right, in the order of elderly woman, young man, elderly woman, young woman. Lou the Rat enters a moment later.*)

NEIGHBORS A AND C (*together*): What are you shouting for?

CH'IN KU-HSIN: An awful thing has happened. There's been a murder!

NEIGHBORS B AND C (*together*): Who's been murdered?

CH'IN KU-HSIN: Somebody's killed Yu Hu-lu!

ALL THE NEIGHBORS (*in unison*): What?

LOU THE RAT: I don't believe it!

(*The neighbors are grouped around Ch'in Ku-hsin at front stage; Lou the Rat is a little apart from them all.*)

CH'IN KU-HSIN: If you don't believe it, go and see.

(*They all enter the shop one after the other and group them-*

selves around the corpse. The young man stands at the head of the corpse looking down at it with his hands on the sash at his waist. The young woman peers in alarm over his right shoulder. One of the elderly women stands between the corpse and the bed, and with a gesture of her right sleeve, duplicates the movement of the pointing right hand of Ch'in Ku-hsin, who indicates the dead man's wound while standing at the feet of the corpse on the opposite side from the neighbor. The second elderly woman stands at some distance from the first, to the rear of Ch'in Ku-hsin. Her right arm is lifted with the hand against her chest, and her left hand grasps the bottom of the right water sleeve. Lou the Rat stands some distance from the alarmed group at the right of the stage to the audience, whom he is facing. His arms are folded across his chest, and with his left hand he strokes his chin in cunning reflection. The neighbors straighten up from looking at the victim and begin to sing in the Huang Lung Kun modal pattern.)

ALL:
   Alas!
   His throat is cut.
   Blood covers his breast.
   His face is like wax.
   His body lies stiff in the dust.
CH'IN KU-HSIN (*pointing*): Look, that meat chopper on the floor is covered with blood!
ALL (*singing again*):
   The murderer killed him with a meat chopper.
LOU THE RAT (*still standing in the same position*): Covered with blood: it frightens a man, eh?
ALL (*speaking in unison*): How did you find out, Uncle Ch'in?
   (*They have regrouped themselves while singing. Ch'in stands within a semicircle formed by the others, with the young woman at the extreme right of the audience and the young man at the extreme left. Lou the Rat moves around to the center of the group facing Ch'in, his back to the corpse, as he speaks.*)
LOU THE RAT: That's right, how did you find out?

CH'IN KU-HSIN (*emphasizing his words with both arms raised, elbows bent at waist height, the water sleeves folded over his wrists*): Last night he came and told me that his relative at Kaoch'iao had lent him fifteen strings of cash. He asked me to go with him to buy a pig today. I came very early this morning to call him, but he was already dead.

NEIGHBOR B: And the fifteen strings of cash?

CH'IN KU-HSIN (*looks around*): Not to be found.

NEIGHBOR C: And his daughter?

CH'IN KU-HSIN: She's disappeared too.

NEIGHBORS (*in unison*): That's very strange!
(*They sing:*)
It's very strange:
The father is dead
And the daughter has gone.
The whole affair looks suspicious.

NEIGHBOR D (*sings*):
The fifteen strings of cash
Caused this calamity.
He was destined to remain poor
And so met a terrible fate.

CH'IN KU-HSIN (*recites in kan-pan*):
Perhaps it was
A dirty thief
That stole his money,
And the wicked scheme accomplished,
Then kidnapped the girl.

NEIGHBOR C (*recites*):
A thief would have brought his own weapon.
To use a meat chopper is very strange.

NEIGHBOR A (*recites*):
Perhaps it was
Su Hsü-chüan
Who killed her father
And ran off with the money.

NEIGHBOR C (*sings*):
Su Hsü-chüan is an upright, honest girl;
How could she act as wickedly as that?

LOU THE RAT (*recites*):
To keep a grown-up girl at home
Is merely storing up trouble.
(*Sings.*)
Su Hsü-chüan must have had a lover.
The two killed the father for his money,
And now the love birds have flown away.

CH'IN KU-HSIN AND THE NEIGHBORS (*reciting in unison*):
But who has ever seen a man in her company?

NEIGHBORS A, B, AND D (*reciting in unison*):
Who indeed has seen her
With a man?
Where was this lover?
(*Lou the Rat bends his knees and rubs his hands one over the other in front of him while he recites.*)

LOU THE RAT:
The proverb says: "When a girl grows up,
So does her heart;
A single existence is hard to bear."
Naturally she would keep it secret.
The man who used the meat chopper
Was no stranger when he committed murder.
She pretended
To be dutiful
While hiding a devil within.
Her hand did the killing.
No need to suspect anyone else.

CH'IN KU-HSIN (*addressing them all*): Whether it was a thief or the girl, whoever did it can't have got very far. Let's split up into two parties.
(*He turns to Neighbors B and D.*)
You two go and inform the magistrate.
(*To Neighbors A and C and Lou the Rat.*)
We'll go and find the murderer.

NEIGHBORS B AND D: Let's go and inform the magistrate. (*They exit.*)

NEIGHBORS A AND C AND CH'IN KU-HSIN: Let's go and find the murderer.
(*They face front with an air of resolution and go off right and*

*left stage after leaving the shop. Lou the Rat remains on stage
in a thoughtful pose, head and body inclined slightly to right.
His right hand is raised, with the index finger of the hand
touching his right cheek. His left arm is lifted in front of
him, elbow bent; his left hand is extended palm inwards,
water sleeve hanging folded from the wrist. He stands re-
flectively for a few moments, then suddenly calls out.)*

LOU THE RAT: I'm coming too; I'm coming too! (*He leaves the
shop and exits right of the stage to the audience.*)
(*Curtain.*)

Scene 2: The Innocent Are Suspected

*Hsiung Yu-lan enters to the left of the audience with fifteen
strings of cash slung over his right shoulder. His gait and posture
are those traditionally used in the role of a young hero (hsiao-sheng
role). His hands are held in front of him, palms uppermost; his
arms are crooked forward from the elbows; his head moves from
side to side with precise but delicately articulated emphasis of
the rhythm. He walks with his feet about six or seven inches apart.
The right foot is lifted forward fourteen inches, and the left foot
then brought up to the right heel at a right angle to it. After a
short pause, during which time he faces the audience, he repeats
the step with an alternate foot movement. As each foot is lifted,
the sole of the shoe is fully revealed. In this fashion Hsiung Yu-lan
sings his way across the stage.*

HSIUNG YU-LAN (*cries out*): I travel along!
(*He begins to sing in the Fen Hai Erh modal pattern.*)
My family is poor,
With little to wear or eat.
It is hard to support my parents.
The days pass in bitterness,
Serving others.
My employer is a wealthy merchant.
I lead a hard life
Buying and selling goods each day

To earn money for my master.
I travel between Suchou and Hangchou
And through the provinces of Hukuang,
Kuangchou, Anhui, Kiangsi and Fukien.[15]
I trade in silk gauze, medicinal herbs,
Mountain products, sea delicacies.
(*Hsiung Hu-lan exits to the right of the audience, and the
curtain is drawn to reveal the second acting area once more.
There is a painted backdrop of a distant mountain landscape,
and scenic trees and foliage flank the exit and entry. This
use of scenery is typical of Chinese traditional theatre today.
   Su Hsü-chüan appears left of the audience. She stands as
though weary, supporting herself with her right hand placed
against the painted tree trunk of the set. Her left hand is
placed against the top of her thigh; her left knee is slightly
bent, heel raised from the floor. She then begins to sing in
the Hung T'iao Yao modal pattern, walking across the stage
as she does so. She takes very short steps—the toe of the
first foot is never more than three inches ahead of the toe
of the second—with her feet parallel and about an inch apart.
The hands are moved slowly across the body from side to
side in the pointing position described on p. 22, emphasizing
the rhythms of the song.*)

SU HSÜ-CHÜAN:
My legs ache, my feet pain me.
(*She stumbles as she moves downstage.*)
My mouth is dry, I'm soaked with sweat;
But I fear they will follow me; I must hurry on.
(*Speaks.*)
I've run until I'm completely exhausted. My head reels,
my eyes are dim. I don't know how much farther it is to
Kaoch'iao. Aiya! How miserable I am.

---

15. Suchou is the Wade romanized form of the more commonly used
Soochow. Hukuang is the old name of a province now divided into Hupeh
and Hunan. Kuangchou is the Wade romanized form for Canton province.
The Wade forms are retained here for consistency in the text.
   The names of the towns and provinces that Hsiung Yu-lan mentions are
single syllables in Chinese, resulting in a special song pattern:
   Tsou pien liao Su, Hang, Hu, Kuang, Huan, Kan, Min.

(*Sings again.*)
A lonely orphan, without family.
A withered leaf, blown in the wind.
Who cares, who thinks of me?
I see one hope before me:
To shelter with my aunt at Kaoch'iao.
I'll confide all my troubles to her.
(*Su Hsü-chüan exits to the right of the audience front stage.
After she leaves the stage, Neighbors A and C cross the sec-
ond acting area from left to right of the audience and disap-
pear in pursuit. Hsiung Yu-lan makes his entry again in the
second acting area as soon as the neighbors have vanished.
He begins to sing in the Fu Ma Liang modal pattern as he
walks slowly across the stage at the rear of the second acting
area.*)

HSIUNG YU-LAN:
I work like an ox or horse, my energy spent
In the end, it's still difficult to support my parents.
Who knows when I can marry
And live happily with a wife?
(*Su Hsü-chüan's voice is heard offstage.*)

SU HSÜ-CHÜAN: You, sir, in front, please wait!

HSIUNG YU-LAN (*turns on hearing the voice and exclaims*): Oh,
it's a young woman!
(*He sings.*)
Does she want to inquire the way?
Why is she all alone?
(*Su Hsü-chüan has now entered and stands with her right leg
placed just behind the left, right toe touching left heel, right
heel off the floor. Her right arm is extended sideways, palm
down, fingers curved in traditional manner as previously described. Her left arm is raised in gesture extended towards
the young merchant, who stands at the rear center stage in
front of the painted backdrop. He has half turned his body,
inclined to the left and supported on his bent left knee. His
left foot points to the right of the audience; his right foot
points towards the audience, the heel about nine inches forward of the left heel. His right arm is lowered and bent
across his waist at the front. His left arm is lowered behind*)

his waist at the left and curved enough to support the water
sleeve in its normal position over the wrist.)

HSIUNG YU-LAN: Why do you call me, miss? Is something the matter?

SU HSÜ-CHÜAN (*sings in the Shua Hai Erh modal pattern*):
Usually I seldom leave the house,
And today I've lost my way, so I'm worried.
That's why I called you.
(*Speaks.*) Please, can you direct me to Kaoch'iao? Which road shall I take?

HSIUNG YU-LAN: Why are you in such a hurry, miss? Is something the matter?
(*Su Hsü-chüan has come up to Hsiung Yu-lan and stands to his right facing front stage, her stance as previously described. Her head is tilted towards the young man; her arms are bent at the elbows. The right hand fingers, outstretched and palm inwards, are placed against her left waist; the left hand is held just in front of the right hand, palm downwards. Hsiung Yu-lan straightens up when the girl approaches and stands squarely facing the audience.*)

SU HSÜ-CHÜAN (*indicating herself*): I'm going to Kaoch'iao in the hope of seeing a relative.

HSIUNG YU-LAN: Why is no one from your family accompanying you?

SU HSÜ-CHÜAN: Because . . . er . . .
(*She recites.*)
Everyone at home is busy;
My parents could not get away.
There's important business, so I must go to Kaoch'iao to find my relative.
I don't know the way: please direct me.

HSIUNG YU-LAN: So that's how it is. Well, if you want to go to Kaoch'iao, miss, I'm actually travelling that way myself. You can go with me. (*As he is talking to her, he points with his left hand right of the stage to the audience. His index finger is extended, the thumb curved against the middle finger, which, along with the fourth and little fingers, is curved inwards to the palm.*)

SU HSÜ-CHÜAN: Thank you very much indeed!

SU HSÜ-CHÜAN AND HSIUNG YU-LAN (*singing in duet*[16]):
I go ahead; He goes ahead.
She drops behind; I drop behind.
Though we travel together, we are strangers,
We are strangers.
We do not ask each other's name;
Why should strangers ask?
(*The voice of Neighbor A is heard offstage.*)
NEIGHBOR A: There are two people in front. I don't know if they
are the murderers. Quick, quick, let's catch them!
SU HSÜ-CHÜAN AND HSIUNG YU-LAN (*singing in unison*):
Suddenly there is shouting.
NEIGHBORS A AND C (*offstage*): Hey, Hey! You two there, slow
down!
SU HSÜ-CHÜAN AND HSIUNG YU-LAN (*singing in unison*):
We see a group of people
Rush madly towards us!
(*Su Hsü-chüan stumbles in her agitation and falls to the floor.
She is still on the floor, resting on her left hand and inclined
towards front stage, but is being helped to her feet by her
companion as their pursuers enter the stage to the left of the
audience. Her right arm is raised and held by Hsiung Yu-
lan, his right hand over her wrist and his left hand under her
arm. He stands directly behind her and leans over to assist
her. The first pursuer to appear is Ch'in Ku-hsin, followed by
Neighbors C and A, the young man and one of the elderly
women, and last of all, Lou the Rat. They pause and stand
in a file peering at the couple. Ch'in Ku-hsin's body is in-*

---

16. Hui Ho Yang modal pattern. This is a duet in six lines with a
syllabic pattern of four, four, seven, three, seven, six. The first two lines
are repeated by each singer, with the first character in the first line meaning "I" (*wo*) or "he" (*t'a*) and the first character in the second line
meaning "she" (*t'a*) or "I" (*wo*), according to the singer:

> (Wo) (T'a) tsai ch'ien hsing
> (T'a) (Wo) tsai hou ken
> T'ung hsin nai shih me lu jen
> Me lu jen
> Tz'u jen hsing ming pu tseng wen
> Me lu jen ho pi wen.

*clined forward, his knees bent; he fingers his beard with his
right hand and holds his left hand at his left waist. The young
man is poised forward on his left foot, right heel raised in
the rear. His left arm is raised at his left waist, his right arm
at his side. The elderly woman peers from behind him, pointing with her right hand, her body slightly bent. Lou the Rat,
a little distance apart from the others, stands with slightly
bent knees, his feet turned out at a forty-five degree angle.
His right arm is bent in front of him at chest height, the index
finger pointing to the upturned palm of his left hand, which
is raised at a slightly lower level than the right. They all
stand looking at the couple. Su Hsü-chüan is by now on her
feet.)*

NEIGHBORS A AND C (*singing in the Feng Ju Sung modal pattern*):
Alas!
We can know men's faces, not their hearts.
We never expected that she
Would have an affair with a murderer.

CH'IN KU-HSIN (*turning towards Su Hsü-chüan*): This is a fine
thing you've done, miss!
(*The old man and the girl are facing each other in front of
the others, who stand in a row watching from behind. Lou
the Rat stands a little apart from the rest, just behind Ch'in
Ku-hsin, his hands clasped together in front of him as he
listens to the conversation with a sly look on his face. Ch'in
leans slightly towards the girl, both arms held in front of him
at waist height, the water sleeves folded over his wrists. Su
Hsü-chüan stands with left arm bent at the elbow, her right
arm extended, and the palm of the right hand upward as she
faces Ch'in. She leans slightly towards her left side, as though
alarmed at Ch'in's fierce demeanor.*)

SU HSÜ-CHÜAN: Uncle Ch'in! I'm going to visit my aunt. What's
wrong with that?

ALL (*singing in unison*):
Your father has been murdered!
(*Su Hsü-chüan steps back one pace with an alarmed air, her
right leg placed just behind the left, right toe touching left
heel, right heel off the floor.*)

SU HSÜ-CHÜAN: What? Father's dead!

ALL (*in chorus*): Of course he's dead!
(*The composition of the group has now changed slightly.
The elderly woman neighbor has moved around to confront
Su Hsü-chüan and emphasizes the last word with a movement of her hands, which are both lifted in front of her at
chest height. Only the extended tips of the fingers of the right
hand, palm downward, are visible beneath the folded water
sleeve; the left hand is hidden within the folded sleeve. She
leans slightly towards the girl, who stands in the posture she
assumed on stepping back one pace. Her right arm is lifted
at right angles in front of her chest, palm down, fingers in
the traditional curved position; her left arm is extended downwards to the left rear, fingers in the curved position; she is
still leaning towards the left, head tilted downwards slightly
to face the neighbor. Lou the Rat is at the extreme rear of
the group to the left of the audience. He has turned away
from the others but is looking backward over his left shoulder
in sly contemplation of events. Hsiung Yu-lan is standing all
this time in surprised contemplation of what is going on. He
is at the extreme right of the group to the audience, with both
hands placed so that the fingers touch either side of his front
waist and with his left foot slightly in front of and oblique
to the right foot. His head movement follows the interchange
of conversation.*
    *After standing for a moment in alarm, Su Hsü-chüan moves
forward as though to go through the group to the entry of
the stage behind them. Ch'in Ku-hsin bars her way. Both his
arms are extended towards the girl's chest, his left foot is in
front of the right, the left arm is higher than the right, and
his head and shoulders are inclined towards the right. Su
Hsü-chüan stands suspended in movement: her left arm is
extended to her rear in line with the left leg, which is poised
on the toes, heel lifted from the floor. Lou the Rat has now
moved around to the front of the group, left foot in front of
right, knees bent a little, and right hand lifted in disapproval.
His whole air is one of exaggerated righteous horror.*)
ALL (*in unison*): Where are you going?
SU HSÜ-CHÜAN: I'm going home to see what has happened.
    (*There is a scornful laugh from everybody.*)

ALL (*singing*):
Your pretense deceives nobody.
SU HSÜ-CHÜAN: If something terrible has happened to Father, why won't you let me go back to see?
ALL (*singing in unison*):
You and your lover killed your father,
Stole his money, and thought to escape.
But now that we've caught the pair of you,
You'll find it hard to escape.
HSIUNG YU-LAN: No wonder she was in such a hurry if that's how it was.
(*He is standing with bowed head as he first speaks, then places both feet together. He holds the bottom of his left sleeve lightly with his right hand and moves the hand, index finger extended upward, in a sweep from the waist to point forward at shoulder height. His head is inclined slightly to the left as this action is completed. He turns to go, but the young man neighbor bars his way. The neighbor stands with right foot thrust forward, knee bent, and left leg extended well to the rear. His left arm is bent and raised at shoulder height, his right arm thrust forward towards Hsiung Yu-lan, palm uppermost. Hsiung stands with his weight resting on his right foot, his left foot a little forward, the heel about six inches in front of the right toe and turned towards the left. His left hand supports the ends of the strings of cash slung over his left shoulder. The rest of the group stand behind Hsiung in a file, bodies inclined slightly to the left, with the exception of Lou the Rat, who steps forward three paces in front of the others to confront Hsiung. Lou the Rat's knees are bent, left foot forward with the heel lifted from the floor. He leans to his right with his shoulders bent forward, and raises his right hand across his chest to point at Hsiung.*)
ALL (*in unison*): Hey! You can't go!
HSIUNG YU-LAN: Why not?
CH'IN KU-HSIN: If you go, who's to be blamed for your crime?
LOU THE RAT (*emphasizing his words with his right hand*): That's right. If you go, do you want me, Lou the Rat, to be blamed?
HSIUNG YU-LAN: This is crazy. What does it have to do with me?

NEIGHBOR C: Don't waste time in talk; let's see if he's got the fifteen strings of cash.

(*The young man and Ch'in Ku-hsin seize the strings of cash from Hsiung, who unavailingly tries to resist them. Ch'in takes the cash and lays them on the floor as he goes down on his knees before them, directly facing the audience. Lou the Rat is standing at Ch'in's right about two feet away and slightly to the rear; his knees are bent, heels apart, toes turned outwards; his hands are lifted in front of him, the right above the left, fingers extended. Both hands are bent forward from the wrist with the fingers towards the floor. His right shoulder is hunched a little higher than the left and his head tilted downwards to the left as he anxiously watches Ch'in Ku-hsin. Directly behind Ch'in, the elderly woman neighbor and Su Hsü-chüan stand facing each other right and left of Ch'in with their profiles to the audience. The elderly woman has both arms lifted in front of her at waist height. Su Hsü-chüan's right arm is bent in front of her breast, hand upright, palm towards the audience in a gesture of protest to her accuser; her left arm is raised so that it is bent at the elbow above her left waist. To her extreme left at the rear, the young man neighbor stands facing the audience, both feet squarely on the floor, the right one forward and the left one placed well to the rear. His hands are lifted at waist height to grasp the extended left arm of Hsiung Yu-lan, who leans forward in a line away from his captor, right foot forward, bending towards Ch'in Ku-hsin and pleading with his right arm outstretched in protest as he calls out.*)

HSIUNG YU-LAN: Hey, hey, that's my money!

ALL (*in unison*): Count it and see, count it and see!

CH'IN KU-HSIN (*counting the cash with his head bent over his task*): Five, ten, fifteen. You see, exactly fifteen, not one string more or less. Do you still want to deny it?

(*He has risen to his feet, and they all confront Hsiung Yu-lan, who turns towards his accusers. His hands are apart, palms upwards, arms held at waist height. Ch'in stands with head and shoulders tilted sharply to his right; his feet are about six inches apart. His left arm is placed across his waist; his right hand, placed just above his left arm, touches the fifteen strings of cash taken from Hsiung Yu-lan and now slung over Ch'in's left shoulder.*)

ALL (*reciting in unison in kan-pan*):

You are a thief, a murderer, and a kidnapper!

A cur with the heart of a wolf!

(*Lou the Rat has come forward from the group and stands before Hsiung Yu-lan. Lou's feet are slightly apart, his knees slightly bent, and his body inclined slightly towards his right. His right hand, fist clenched but with the thumb pointing, is raised at shoulder height towards Hsiung.*)

LOU THE RAT (*sings*):

So evil an heart—

So cowardly a deed—

You dastardly murderer!

HSIUNG YU-LAN: Gentlemen, wait a minute! My name is Hsiung Yu-lan, and I am employed by the merchant T'ao Fu-chu. My master gave me these fifteen strings of cash to go to Ch'angchou to buy wooden combs. I've never seen this young woman before: how can you accuse me of murder?

SU HSÜ-CHÜAN (*from the background*): I've never met this gentleman before. You cannot wrong an innocent man!

ALL (*in unison*): That's what you say. How do we know whether you are telling the truth or lying?

HSIUNG YU-LAN: My master T'ao Fu-chu is staying at the Yüeh-lai Inn in front of the Hsüan Miao Temple at Suchou. If you people don't believe me, please send somebody to go and find out!

(*They all look at each other, not quite knowing what to think.*)

ALL (*reciting in unison*):

To doubt his words—

To believe his words—

It is hard to know.

Are they true or false?

This affair is difficult to explain

And difficult to decide.

LOU THE RAT (*fearful at this doubt, emphasizes his accusation*):

Here are the guilty pair. If they didn't kill Yu Hu-lu, it's
hard to know who did!

(*Two runners from the magistrate's court enter, accompanied
by the other two neighbors, B and D, the elderly woman and
the young woman. Lou the Rat points to Hsiung Yu-lan.*)
Here are the murderers! Arrest them quickly!

(*The two runners seize Hsiung Yu-lan and Su Hsü-chüan,
shackling their wrists with chains.*)

RUNNERS AND NEIGHBORS (*reciting in unison in kan-pan*):
When a man is murdered,
It's a life for a life.
Those who kill must be killed.

RUNNERS (*to the prisoners*): Forward!

CH'IN KU-HSIN AND NEIGHBORS (*in unison*): Wait a minute, wait
a minute! We've still got to get to the bottom of this!

FIRST RUNNER: Never mind about that: it will soon be settled in
court!

SECOND RUNNER: Forward! The rest of you had better come too!

ALL (*together*): All right; all right.

(*All except Lou the Rat file offstage to the right of the audience. He remains standing and looking furtively from side to
side before finally following the others.*)
(*Curtain.*)

Scene 3: Wrongly Accused

*The curtain is drawn to reveal the Wuhsi District Court. Plate 6
gives a clear idea of the setting, which is placed in the second
acting area. On the magistrate's table are a large cube wrapped in
yellow silk, representing the Imperial Seal, and a vase containing
ink brushes. Four court attendants enter to the left of the audience. Two of the attendants place themselves at either side of the
magistrate's dais; a third stands at the extremity of the fence that
marks the petitioner's entry to the court.*

*The district magistrate, Kuo Yü-chih, attended by the fourth
court runner, makes his entry with a proud and haughty gait. This*

is a lao-sheng role, in which the actor's technique symbolizes a scholar or official of mature age. His hands, over which are folded the water sleeves, grasp the jade girdle at either side. As the actor walks, his legs are straight and his waist rigid, and he looks straight ahead, with his head erect. As he pauses for each step, there is a short, precise movement of the head to alternate sides. The actor's steps are what is known as "square," that is, from side to side giving a very characteristic style of progression. Initially, both feet are placed squarely on the floor six or seven inches apart. The right foot is then lifted forward fourteen inches and the left foot brought up to the right heel and at right angles to it. The actor pauses, and the movement is repeated with the left foot forward first, and so on. In this fashion, the magistrate takes himself to the center rear of the stage, so that he is standing a few feet in front of the extreme point of the fence which marks the boundary of the court on the set, and turns to face the audience. Kuo Yü-chih places both hands, with thumbs beneath and the fingers close together but extended, on top of the front portion of his beard, slowly and deliberately sweeping it from top to bottom. As he completes this gesture, he addresses the audience.

KUO YÜ-CHIH (*recites*):
> I fear the people here are a troublesome lot;
> What with harpies and scamps, we have much litigation.
> (*As he begins to speak, he holds both hands in front of him just above waist level, right palm upturned, left hand holding the right water sleeve; he turns obliquely to the right while reciting the two lines above. In the final position his right hand is extended palm upwards, thumb apart. For the next two lines he turns obliquely left, left hand still holding the right water sleeve; but in the final position his right thumb is placed against the bent second, third, and fourth fingers, the index finger being extended.*)
> To preserve the peace, I govern strictly
> And award severe punishments to enforce the law.
> (*He now faces the audience, hands still in the same position, before he begins a series of gestures to emphasize his spoken words.*)
> Since I came to Wuhsi, I have repeatedly encountered diffi-

cult cases. Luckily, although the people have been crafty by
nature, with my powers of investigation and cross-examina-
tion, I can decide nine out of ten cases.

(*As he speaks these words, he holds his head high and with
right hand indicates himself. The palm is turned down and
the thumb extended inwards as indicator.*)

From the governor himself down to the ordinary citizen, is
there anyone who does not recognize my shrewd powers of
deduction?

(*As he finishes these words, his head is thrown back haughtily, and he faces right. His left hand is dropped to hold the
jade girdle; and his right hand—palm down, fingers curled,
the little finger higher than the rest, and thumb and little
finger together—makes a gesture of emphasis at chest height.
For the following passage he raises both hands with palms
inwards and fingers widely extended from each other; and
with the index finger and thumb of each hand, he caresses
the two outer strands of his beard from the ear downwards
and outwards.*)

Today, I am trying the murderers of Yu Hu-lu. They have
already been arrested, and now I must take my seat in Court.
(*He calls out.*) Come! Open the Court.

ATTENDANTS (*in unison*): Your Honor!

(*Kuo Yü-chih turns and walks in stately fashion, his path
like an inverted S, to the seat behind the table on the dais,
which is at the extreme right of the stage to the audience. He
stands squarely behind the table and then seats himself, knees
wide apart, hands on the jade girdle.*)

KUO YÜ-CHIH: Bring the neighbors into Court!

(*The attendant at the extreme left of the set to the audience
repeats the call.*)

ATTENDANT: Bring the neighbors into Court!

(*The neighbors, including Lou the Rat, appear one after the
other from behind the fence of the court and stand rather
fearfully before the magistrate. Ch'in Ku-hsin is in front of
the group, and behind him are ranged the young woman, the
two elderly women, and the young man. Lou the Rat is
nearest the audience, and as always, a little apart from the
others. They all go down on their knees, their heads bowed.*)

NEIGHBORS (*in unison*): We pay our respects, Sir!

KUO YÜ-CHIH: You are all Yu Hu-lu's neighbors, are you not?

NEIGHBORS (*lifting their heads*): Yes.

KUO YÜ-CHIH: Stand up to answer!

NEIGHBORS (*rising to their feet in a group*): Yes, Sir! (*They stand erect facing the magistrate, hands held at waist height in front of them, the young man with feet together, the young woman with her right leg crossed behind her left leg in the stance previously described for Su Hsü-chüan after she calls to Hsiung at the beginning of Scene 2. Lou the Rat, his knees slightly bent and feet apart, faces the audience; his right hand is closed over his left in front of him at chest height, and his head is inclined over his left shoulder towards the magistrate's desk.*)

KUO YÜ-CHIH: How did you know that Yu Hu-lu had been murdered, and how did you catch the two murderers?

CH'IN KU-HSIN (*steps forward half a pace and answers, emphasizing his description with his right hand*): Your Excellency, it was like this. After borrowing fifteen strings of cash from a relative at Kaoch'iao, Yu Hu-lu came to see me yesterday evening and asked me to go with him to help buy a pig. I feared he might oversleep because he was drunk, so I went to call him early but found he had been murdered. His daughter Su Hsü-chüan had disappeared. A few of us reported the matter officially, and the rest of us went off to catch the murderers. We were hurrying towards Kaoch'iao when we suddenly saw Su Hsü-chüan walking along in the company of a man; that man had exactly fifteen strings of cash on him . . . (*At these words he turns toward the audience, his head towards the rest of the neighbors, both hands held in front of him at waist height but hidden by the hanging water sleeves.*)

KUO YÜ-CHIH: Ah, so the money that Hsiung Yu-lan was carrying amounted to exactly fifteen strings of cash, did it?

NEIGHBORS (*in unison*): Yes!

KUO YÜ-CHIH: They were walking together, were they . . .

(*He ponders. The neighbors stand waiting expectantly.*)

Therefore, it is evident that Hsiung Yu-lan and Su Hsü-chüan plotted this murder. There is no question about it.

NEIGHBORS (*in unison with the exception of Lou the Rat*): This
. . . we hardly dare say.

LOU THE RAT (*stepping forward to the magistrate's desk, left foot
forward, hands placed on thighs, body inclined towards the
magistrate sitting above him*): If His Honor says they plotted the murder, then of course they plotted the murder!

KUO YÜ-CHIH: Right! Leave the Court.

LOU THE RAT: Ah! Your Excellency is truly a shrewd judge! Ah, a
shrewd judge! (*As he repeats his flattery, he is facing the
audience. His raised left hand, with fingers clenched and
thumb pointing up, is tilted towards the magistrate; and he
holds his left water sleeve with his right hand. He then turns
and goes quickly off after the others.*)

KUO YÜ-CHIH: Come! Bring Su Hsü-chüan into Court!

ATTENDANT (*passing on the order*): Bring Su Hsü-chüan into
Court!

(*She appears between two other attendants, goes down on
her knees, and makes her obeisance before the magistrate.*)

FIRST ATTENDANT: Here are the stolen fifteen strings of cash. (*He
places them on the magistrate's desk.*)

SU HSÜ-CHÜAN (*her head still bowed*): I pay my respects to Your
Honor.

KUO YÜ-CHIH: Look at me!

SU HSÜ-CHÜAN: I dare not raise my head.

KUO YÜ-CHIH: If I tell you to raise your head, then raise your
head!

(*She raises her head slowly to look at the magistrate. She
leans backward slightly, body inclined to her right, right arm
extended downwards, left arm across her chest, hands with
fingers in the position previously described on p. 67. Kuo
Yü-chih sits with his head tilted sharply to the right; both
hands are lifted from the table, palms upwards, index fingers
extended, second, third, and fourth fingers closed.*)

Pretty as the peach and the plum blossom—how could she
not have attracted a lover! (*He raises his head to face right
of the audience, his eyes still turned on the girl. His right
hand, fist closed, palm downwards, is brought over his left
hand, which is lowered although still in its former position.*)

In the springtime of life, how could she remain cold and

without passion? (*He again faces the girl squarely over his desk, his eyes narrowed and his hands lowered.*) Of course she had a lover and wanted to run away with him. (*He places both hands before him on the desk, tilts his head slightly to his right, and faces left of the audience again.*) The father tried to prevent her, so she killed him and stole his money—it's obvious. There's no need to ask what happened. I can tell beforehand. (*He raises his right fist in a gesture of decision in front of him; his head is straightened but still facing right of the audience.*) Su Hsü-chüan, why did you plot with that scoundrel to steal fifteen strings of cash, kill your father, and run away?

su hsü-chüan: Your Excellency, I did not do a single one of the things you say.

(*She has moved nearer to the desk. Kuo Yü-chih bends over the desk towards the girl, his right hand holding the edge of the desk; his left arm is crooked in a right angle, with the first and second fingers of the left hand extended to point at the girl. Su Hsü-chüan turns her head away from him to face the audience, but her body is inclined towards the magistrate, right leg behind the left. Her bent right arm is placed across her chest, palm towards the magistrate, fingers extended. Her left hand is held in an identical position, with the arm extended left towards the magistrate. She repeats piteously:*) Your Excellency! I did not do a single one of the things you say!

(*Su Hsü-chüan sinks to her knees again. Kuo Yü-chih half rises to lean across the desk, grasps the bottom of his beard with his left hand, and points at her with the extended first and second fingers of his right hand.*)

kuo yü-chih: Ah, ah! She denies it and says she is innocent! I have another question for you. Your father's name was Yu. Why are you called Su?

su hsü-chüan (*kneeling upright, her left arm bent at her lower left side, fingers in position, and her right arm held across her chest as she indicates herself*): My father died when I was a small child. When my mother married again, she took me along, but I retained my father's name.

KUO YÜ-CHIH (*sitting down again but still leaning forward over his desk, his right index finger and second finger lifted in admonition, a sneer on his face*): There you are! You were not his own daughter, and when he saw you flirting and bringing trouble on his good name, he naturally tried to correct your behavior. That was when you hated him in your heart and first thought of killing him. Wasn't that so?

SU HSÜ-CHÜAN (*firmly*): I did no such thing!

KUO YÜ-CHIH: How can that be true? The proverb runs, "To catch a thief, first take him with his loot; to call a woman a deceiver, first catch her with a lover." Today the pair of you have been caught; we also have the fifteen strings of cash and the neighbors' proof. With such complete evidence, how can you possibly think you are unjustly accused!

SU HSÜ-CHÜAN: I really think I am unjustly accused:

(*She turns on her knees to face right of the audience. Her left arm is bent, the hand raised before her at chest height, palm towards her right. The thumb and middle finger touch; the other fingers are raised, with the little finger the highest. The right hand, fingers curled in the same way, is held slightly below the left wrist. This is the kind of gesture that only the trained actress can make with delicacy and grace. Su Hsü-chüan now begins to sing a lament in the Chi Yen Hui modal pattern, a characteristic technique used in women's roles for a trial scene.*)

My father, desiring money,
Sold my body.
I don't wish to be a slave
So I absconded.
I lost my way,
And a young gentleman stranger on the road
Offered to accompany me.
I was falsely suspected.
Escaping one calamity, I find another injustice
Has descended from Heaven upon me!

KUO YÜ-CHIH: A lot of nonsense! Just now the neighbors said your father borrowed fifteen strings of cash from a relative. Yet you accuse him of selling you—clearly, these are malicious

words to injure others. In spite of your youth, you are cruel
and without shame, a hardened murderer. But I think I've
dealt with worse cases than this! I don't care how crafty you
are! Do you think you can still deceive a magistrate like me?
(*His head is inclined sharply to his right, his hands clasped
in front of him. He finally brings his right hand down sharply
on the desk and leans angrily over his desk towards the girl,
who is kneeling with bent head again.*)

SU HSÜ-CHÜAN: Heavens! (*She falls backwards leaning sharply
towards her right, her right leg bent under her, her head tilted
upward towards the magistrate. Her left leg is extended
straight in front of her off the floor, toes pointing vertically;
her arms are bent and held in front of her body as though
warding off a blow, the left hand being the distance of the left
forearm from the wrist at the right arm. Fingers are extended and held vertically, palms outward.*)

KUO YÜ-CHIH (*reciting in kan-pan*):
You killed your father, stole his money;
Still you desire to show your cunning.
I see that if you are not punished severely,
You will continue to deny it!

SU HSÜ-CHÜAN: I've nothing to confess!

KUO YÜ-CHIH: Come! Drag her away and take her up to the thumb-
screws!
(*Three of the court attendants stride forward, the two on
either side of the magistrate's desk leaning forward on bent
left knees, hands clasped together in front of them across
their waists, while the attendant at the entry stands posing,
elbows crooked, fists clenched, right fist at shoulder height,
left at the waist. They seize the girl and drag her out. The
first court attendant reappears.*)

FIRST ATTENDANT: The girl cannot endure it. She's fainted!

KUO YÜ-CHIH: Stop the punishment!

FIRST ATTENDANT (*calling out*): Stop the punishment!
(*Two attendants drag Su Hsü-chüan in and throw her to the
floor. She sits facing the audience, right leg tucked under her,
left leg extended on the floor, knee bent, to her left. She holds
her hands before her, palms inward, just below face level.
The two attendants stand behind threateningly. The one at*

*her left stands leaning towards the prisoner, with his left
hand behind his back, right arm by his side, left leg thrust
straight back, and his weight on his right foot. The one at
her right stands with legs wide apart, right knee bent to support his weight, and left arm crooked with the hand on his
left waist. His right arm, bent from the elbow, is thrust forward at waist height, and he has a writing brush in his right
hand.)*

KUO YÜ-CHIH: Order her to sign her deposition!

*(The attendant at her left draws out a scroll of paper, and
extending it tightly held by both hands, leans towards the
girl with his right knee bent and left leg extended directly to
his rear. The second attendant grasps the prisoner's right
hand with his left hand, and leaning forward on his right
bent knee, holds the writing brush poised aloft in front of
him, slightly above shoulder height. Su Hsü-chüan is looking
at him fearfully.)*

ATTENDANT: Sign your deposition!

*(Because Su Hsü-chüan's hands are numb from torture, she
cannot hold the pen. The attendant grasps her hand and
forces her to make a thumbprint on the paper held by the
other attendant.)*

KUO YÜ-CHIH: Take her away, fasten her in chains, and put her in
jail.

(The attendants drag Su Hsü-chüan off and quickly return.)

KUO YÜ-CHIH: Bring that wicked fellow into Court!

*(The attendants go off and return dragging Hsiung Yu-lan,
who goes down on his knees in front of the magistrate's desk.
The attendants step back; there are two to the left and two
to the right of the magistrate's dais. The prisoner is manacled
with chains.)*

HSIUNG YU-LAN *(with bowed head)*: I pay my respects to you,
Sir!

KUO YÜ-CHIH *(sitting bolt upright)*: Hsiung Yu-lan! You con-
spired with Su Hsü-chüan, stole fifteen strings of cash, and
murdered Yu Hu-lu. Yet you still do not confess!

HSIUNG YU-LAN: Sir, I beg you to hear my petition.

*(He begins to sing, still on bended knees, in the Ch'i Yen
Hui modal pattern.)*

The day before yesterday I arrived from Suchou
On my way to buy goods in Ch'angchou.
That girl had lost her way,
So I accompanied her to show her the road.
I had never seen her before in all my life
And never had a love affair.
The fifteen strings of cash were to buy merchandise.
When could I have committed this crime?
(*His right arm is forward, elbow crooked at a right angle;
his left arm is extended at shoulder height, index finger and
middle finger extended as pointers.*)

KUO YÜ-CHIH (*leaning back in his seat, his body inclined to his
left*): You have the gift of the gab: you can certainly talk.
(*He leans forward, left hand raised from the wrist, fingers
extended.*) But who is going to believe you? (*Still leaning
forward, he grasps his beard with his left hand, right hand on
his desk.*) You say you were on your way from Suchou to
Ch'angchou, but how was it you met Su Hsü-chüan just at
the right time? (*Kuo Yü-chih has relaxed a little in his seat.
He holds his right hand, index finger and middle finger extended, in front of him just above the desk. He keeps his feet
wide apart all the time, the traditional sitting posture for a
male character.*) You say you had never seen her before in
your life: why, then, was she not walking with somebody else,
why was it you in particular that she accompanied? You say
the fifteen strings of cash were to buy merchandise: why was
the sum exactly the same as the sum stolen from Yu Hu-lu?
Su Hsü-chüan has already admitted the truth. You had better
confess quickly!
(*Kuo Yü-chih has swung around slightly to his left, his
shoulders at an angle, left slightly higher than the right, head
tilted in the same way. His right arm is bent across and above
the desk, index and middle fingers of the right hand extended
pointing to his left. His left hand is placed on his left knee.
His eyes are fixed on Hsiung Yu-lan, who turns to face the
audience on his bended knees, his chained hands held in front
of him, palms upward, in supplication.*)

HSIUNG YU-LAN: I have nothing to confess!

KUO YÜ-CHIH (*sitting bolt upright, hands on knees*): Come! Take
him away. Give him forty heavy strokes!

(*Two attendants seize the prisoner, and the three assume a pose. Hsiung has his head thrown back in defiance and is inclined at an angle to the audience, right knee bent, left leg thrust straight forward. His arms are outstretched left and right. One attendant, head turned toward the prisoner, grasps Hsiung's left wrist and supports his left arm from the rear while pulling backwards. The second attendant is directly behind Hsiung's outflung right arm, which the attendant is holding with both hands.*)

HSIUNG YU-LAN (*defiantly*): Beat me to death, but you will not get a confession!

(*Kuo Yü-chih rises to lean over the table, grasps his beard with his left hand, and with his right hand seizes an ink brush, which he holds poised over his desk in front of him. He speaks angrily.*)

KUO YÜ-CHIH: What!

(*He recites in kan-pan.*)

Small punishments may be endured;

Great punishment is difficult to bear.

If you do not confess,

The ankle squeezers wait for you.

HSIUNG YU-LAN: I am being wronged!

KUO YÜ-CHIH (*sitting upright again*): Come! Inflict heavy punishment!

ATTENDANTS (*in unison*): Yes, Sir! (*Two of them drag Hsiung Yu-lan off.*)

FIRST ATTENDANT (*reentering*): The criminal has fainted!

KUO YÜ-CHIH: Stop the punishment!

FIRST ATTENDANT (*calling out*): Stop the punishment!

(*Two attendants drag Hsiung Yu-lan back onstage and throw him to the floor in front of the magistrate. He leans backwards facing the magistrate, his left leg extended fully and his right leg doubled beneath him, supporting himself on his right arm, elbow bent, hand squarely on the floor. His left arm is placed across his bent right leg. He sings a lament in the Ch'ien Ch'iang modal pattern.*)

HSIUNG YU-LAN:

For accompanying her, I am suspected of crime.

It is a calamity descended suddenly out of the sky.

The torture is hard to bear!

ATTENDANTS (*pointing at Hsiung Yu-lan*): Confess!
(*The prisoner remains silent.*)
KUO YÜ-CHIH (*raising his right arm to head height, the upper arm at a right angle to his body, his right hand hidden within the water sleeve, which hangs down vertically*): Tell him to sign!
ATTENDANTS: Sign!
(*One of the attendants thrusts an ink brush at Hsiung Yu-lan, and he seizes it angrily, holding it in his right fist, palm upturned in front of his face. The attendant who has forced the brush on the prisoner stands to Hsiung's left rear with his right arm upraised and fist clenched. Another attendant stands directly behind the prisoner, leaning towards him, with his right leg bent forward. A third attendant stands to the right of Hsiung, his right arm akimbo, his left fist clenched and held forward. He stands with right leg thrust forward and slightly bent, and left leg outstretched and thrust to the rear. The fourth attendant stands directly to Hsiung Yu-lan's left, lunging towards him on his bent right leg, the left leg fully extended to the rear. He holds the bottom of an unrolled paper scroll with his outstretched right hand, grasping the other end with his left hand, which is drawn sharply back. The group stands poised like this in tableau.*)
HSIUNG YU-LAN: Hateful injustice deep as the ocean!
(*The attendants seize his wrist and force him to sign the confession.*)
KUO YÜ-CHIH (*sitting back in his seat*): Come! Take him away, fasten him in chains, and put him in jail!
(*Hsiung Yu-lan is dragged off by two of the attendants. The other two stand at the alert on either side of the magistrate's dais.*)
KUO YÜ-CHIH (*throwing back his head, his body half turned towards the audience, and bursting into a staccato laugh*): Ho, ho, ho! That's how I solve an important law case. In a few words I can make it perfectly clear, and intelligible. (*He leans forward slightly, head lowered again, hands resting on his desk.*) Truly, if a man has great talents, it is simple enough once he has made the right beginning. The Court may withdraw!
(*Curtain.*)

Scene 4: Sentenced to Execution

The first part of this scene takes place in the stage area before the second curtain, with no other setting. It represents the entry to the Suchou prefecture jail. Two executioners enter left of the audience. They stride to the front stage center and recite.

FIRST EXECUTIONER: I carry the executioner's sword,

SECOND EXECUTIONER: To behead criminals.

EXECUTIONERS (*calling out in unison*): Open the gate! Open the gate!

(*The voice of a jailer is heard offstage.*)

JAILER: I'm coming. (*He comes onstage to the right of the audience and goes through the pantomime of opening the jail door.*) Oh, so it's you two! What do you want?

EXECUTIONERS: The governor wants Prefect K'uang to deal with the two criminals in custody tonight. We two have come to bind Hsiung Yu-lan and escort him to the execution ground.

JAILER: Wait a minute, sirs.

(*The two executioners go off right of the audience as the jailer cries out.*)

Hsiung Yu-lan, get a move on there!

HSIUNG YU-LAN (*crying out offstage*): Aiya! What bitter affliction.

(*He begins to sing, still offstage.*[17])

Meeting with such strange injustice,

I feel enraged; it is difficult to keep calm.

(*He enters the stage, hands manacled.*) I hate that stupid official.

JAILER: Hsiung Yu-lan, congratulations![18]

(*Hsiung Yu-lan stands center stage in an attitude of agony. His hands are held up before him in their chains, his head is swung down to the right, the horsehair plume hanging down in front.*)

---

17. In the Chih San Hsing modal pattern, here, a two-line verse with a syllabic grouping of three, four in each line and a rhyming ending for each grouping.

Tsao ch'i yuan, pei fen nan p'ing
Hen hun kuan, luan ting tsui ming

18. A convention for notifying a prisoner of the capital sentence.

HSIUNG YU-LAN (*sings*):
  Hearing those words, I shudder!
  Surely it's . . . Surely it's . . .
  (*The jailer is to the right of the prisoner, his hands clasped in front of him across his waist. He stands with feet apart and knees slightly bent.*)
JAILER: Though a man live to be a hundred, he has to die sometime. You should not worry too much!
  (*Hsiung Yu-lan flings back his head, sweeping the plume to hang down his back. He stands with head uplifted and mancled hands raised towards heaven. His feet are wide apart, his knees slightly bent.*)
HSIUNG YU-LAN (*sings*):
  If I am killed unjustly,
  How shall I close my eyes in peace?
JAILER: It's like this now: the Wuhsi district magistrate passed judgment, the Ch'angchou prefect confirmed it, and the authorities in the capital have ordered your execution—three final decisions; the case is already closed. Even if you declare it unjust, it will be difficult to alter it.
HSIUNG YU-LAN (*singing*):
  I don't know what destiny has destroyed my peaceful way of life!
  Who will look after my parents, that aged, white-haired couple?
JAILER: If you had been tried by our Suchou prefect K'uang, there would have been no injustice. Our prefect K'uang loves his people like his own children; he is the new Pao Ch'eng.[19] Today he is going to superintend the execution.
  (*The jailer leans towards his prisoner; his hands are held in front of him at chest height, right hand over left. Hsiung Yu-lan is bent forward again, his hands held down in front of him, his head tilted to the right, plume hanging down over his right shoulder.*)
HSIUNG YU-LAN: The prefect is going to supervise the execution?
JAILER: That's right.

---

19. Pao Ch'eng, or Kung, a celebrated statesman-scholar of the eleventh century A.D., was famed for his just verdicts and fair dealings as an official.

HSIUNG YU-LAN (*throwing back his head and singing*):
I only wish he would discover the injustice
And bring a dead man back to life.

JAILER: He has only been ordered to supervise the execution, not to question the authority of judgment. Even if he knew you had been unjustly sentenced, he could do nothing about it.

EXECUTIONERS (*calling offstage*): Quick, let's go, let's go!

JAILER: Coming!

(*He grasps Hsiung's chains and leads him, protesting and dragging his feet reluctantly, offstage.*)

(*The second curtain is raised to show the Suchou prefectural court. The setting, shown in Plate 7, again consists of fussy detail which is unnecessary overstatement by all the traditional standards. It is placed against the rear curtain so that the action is played directly in front of the audience instead of in the right half of the stage, as with the Wuhsi District Court scene.*

Four court attendants enter and range themselves at the rear of the stage on either side of the dais. They are followed by the prefect's personal assistant, who walks to the front of the dais and stands there with his hands placed behind his back.

Prefect K'uang Chung next enters. He crosses to center stage and takes his position, facing the audience, in front of his assistant. He stands with right foot placed obliquely and in front of the left. With his right sleeve, he performs the tou-hsiu gesture: his right hand, palm inward, is swept downwards from the chest to the right knee, and with a turn of the wrist, the water sleeve is flung backwards and a little to the right. The water sleeve is then flicked into position to hang over the wrist as the arm is drawn up to waist height again. At the same time, he caresses his beard with his left hand, using a downward movement to the left. He then sings in the Tien Chiang Ch'un modal pattern.)

K'UANG CHUNG:
Strictly upholding the law,
Kind yet stern,
I sympathize with the people's troubles

And investigate their conditions.
I always desire to imitate
The example of Pao Ch'eng.
(*Speaking.*) I, K'uang Chung, since becoming prefect of
Suchou have seen the crops ripe and abundant and the people
happy. I have received an order from above to supervise the
execution of two criminals tonight. The executioners have already arrived with the prisoners. (*As he speaks, he raises
both hands at temple height on either side, palms inward,
eyes focussed upwards. He then brings his hands down to
chest height, finger tips touching, and looks directly to the
front. Finally, he holds his arms forward, slightly bent at
waist height, the water sleeves pendant over the wrists.*)

EXECUTIONERS (*offstage*): Get along there!

(*K'uang Chung takes his seat on the dais in the same way as
described for Kuo Yü-chih in Scene 3 and sits with his feet
wide apart. His assistant takes up a position directly to
K'uang's left rear, standing erect, arms behind his back. Four
executioners enter, leading Hsiung Yu-lan and Su Hsü-chüan.
As the executioners make their entry, they call out, announc-
ing themselves.*)
The criminals enter; the criminals are before you!
(*The two prisoners go down on their knees before the prefect, Hsiung Yu-lan to the right of the audience and Su
Hsü-chüan to the left. Their backs are to the audience, but
they kneel obliquely to the dais. The four executioners stand
at attention, hands on hips, at a short distance to the right
and left of the prisoners and facing the audience.*)

HSIUNG YU-LAN AND SU HSÜ-CHÜAN (*in unison, raising their manacled hands in supplication towards the prefect*): Honored
Sir! Injustice! Save our lives!

K'UANG CHUNG (*raising his right hand and indicating the prisoners
with his first and middle fingers*): What!
(*He sings in the Hun Chiang Lung modal pattern.*)
The murderer, according to the law,
Must pay with his life.
This is clearly and irrevocably stated
In the Canons of the Law.

(*Speaks.*) Raise your heads!
(*He points at the prisoners with the index and middle fingers of his left hand. Two executioners step forward and brusquely tilt the prisoners' bent heads towards the magistrate. K'uang Chung again sings.*)
You should have been loyal, hard-working people,
And not have indulged in wicked conduct as thieves.
Because you have broken the laws of man and Heaven,
You must suffer the extreme penalty.
(*The two executioners push the prisoners' heads down again. K'uang Chung resumes singing.*)
How sad
When lustful people must be punished with death.
It is laughable
When greed for money ruins lives!
(*Speaks.*) Take off their shackles!
(*Two executioners remove the chains from the prisoners' wrists. The man and the girl, who are leaning backwards and supported by the arms of the executioners, are offered wine to drink but refuse it. The two prisoners then sink to the floor, he leaning backwards supported on his left arm, she on her right. His left leg is doubled under him and right leg outstretched; her right is doubled under and left outstretched.*)
Take off their outer garments and bind them!
(*The executioners raise the prisoners to their feet and bind their hands behind their backs. The prisoners stand obliquely to the audience, heads facing the prefect; Su Hsü-chüan's left leg, heel poised, is placed behind the right; Hsiung Yu-lan's right foot is thrust squarely forward beyond his left foot and at right angles to it. The prefect has risen in his seat and stands with his hands at waist height, the right hand with fingers extended towards the prisoners.*)
The law must be strict with wicked people. If there are evil tendencies, how can it be lenient?
HSIUNG YU-LAN AND SU HSÜ-CHÜAN (*in unison*): Honored Sir!
HSIUNG YU-LAN: The wrong done me is higher than a mountain.
SU HSÜ-CHÜAN: The wrong done me is deeper than the sea!
K'UANG CHUNG: You talk too much!

ATTENDANTS (*in unison*): You talk too much!

K'UANG CHUNG (*singing*):

If you were wronged, how was your crime established?
If you were wronged, how are there witnesses to prove it?
Executioners!

(*They step forward.*)

Wait until the fifth watch is struck in the drum tower——

HSIUNG YU-LAN AND SU HSÜ-CHÜAN (*in unison, their voices full of pleading*): Honored Sir!

K'UANG CHUNG (*singing*):

Draw your swords and raise them at the ready!

(*The executioners draw their swords.*)

To quickly strike off their heads on the order!

(*He sits and his assistant hands him the order for execution. The prefect takes an ink brush from the holder on the desk in front of him and holds it poised as Hsiung Yu-lan leans towards him, pleading in unison with Su Hsü-chüan.*)

HSIUNG YU-LAN AND SU HSÜ-CHÜAN: Honored Sir!

(*The two go down on their knees. The executioners are about to silence them, but the prefect checks them with a glance.*)

HSIUNG YU-LAN: Everyone says you love the people like your own children, that you are a second Pao Ch'eng. If that is so, it is difficult to know why you accept the Court's wrong decision and let me die unjustly.

SU HSÜ-CHÜAN: If you execute good people, how can you think you are a just official or say you love your people.

(*The executioners call her to order but are checked once more by the prefect.*)

K'UANG CHUNG: Think how many courts you have been through— three trials and six interrogations. The case is already closed. You two people still continue to insist you are innocent, but it is difficult to believe that without evidence. If you have been wronged, prove it!

HSIUNG YU-LAN: Honored Sir! I was sentenced for conspiring to commit murder with this girl, but it's not true! There's no proof!

K'UANG CHUNG: How can you confirm that there's no proof and it's not true?

HSIUNG YU-LAN: My home is at Huaian, her home is in Wuhsi.

The two of us had never met before she lost her way. I offered to direct her along the road, but does that mean we had an immoral affair? I travel for the merchant T'ao Fu-chu the year round, buying and selling local products. The fifteen strings of cash I carried were given me by my master to buy wooden combs in Ch'angchou. How could I have stolen them?

K'UANG CHUNG: Where is your master, T'ao Fu-chu, now?

HSIUNG YU-LAN: When I left, he was staying at the Yüeh-lai Inn in front of the Taoist temple in this city. He was waiting until I returned with the goods, and then we were both going to Fukien to sell them. Sir, if you don't believe me, please send someone to go and ask him.

(*K'uang Chung ponders and strokes his beard downwards with his right hand.*)

SU HSÜ-CHÜAN: I had never met this young gentleman before, but I was going to Kaoch'iao to see a relative and lost the way, so I asked him for direction and he was suspected and sentenced to death although he's done nothing wrong; I got him into this trouble. Honored Sir! If you can find out where this gentleman comes from, you will know that we are being wronged when we are accused of plotting murder together!

K'UANG CHUNG (*writing out an order and turning to his assistant*): Here! Go quickly to the Yüeh-lai Inn in front of the Taoist temple and verify this matter!

(*The assistant takes the order and goes off. K'uang Chung picks up documents and studies them. The prisoners remain kneeling, their heads deeply bowed. K'uang Chung rises to his feet.*)

One lived in Huaian; one lived in Wuhsi.

(*Sings in the T'ien Hsia Lo modal pattern.*)

How could they be lovers?

One was going to Ch'angchou; one was going to Kaoch'iao.

(*He raises his left hand palm outwards, fingers extended, towards Su Hsü-chüan as he sings; his right foot is placed forward resting on the heel, the toe of his boot turned outward and upwards. He then changes his position to the right hand and left foot as he faces towards Hsiung Yu-lan.*)

They could still be travelling together.

There is no real proof of these two people's guilt.
It's hard to say whether Hsiung Yu-lan's
Fifteen strings of cash were for goods or not.
When everything is so indefinite in this murder case,
How was it possible to pass the death sentence
Without discriminating between black and white?
(*The assistant returns and goes up to the prefect's dais.*)

ASSISTANT: Your Honor! I have just been to make inquiries and have verified this matter. T'ao Fu-chu has already left for Fukien on business. The innkeeper says that this Hsiung Yu-lan is really the assistant of T'ao Fu-chu, who actually gave him the fifteen strings of cash to buy merchandise in Ch'angchou. This is the register from the Yüeh-lai Inn: please look at it, Your Honor!

(*He hands the prefect the book he carries in his left hand. K'uang Chung is turned towards his assistant, his left hand placed on the desk before him; his right hand caresses his beard downward to the right and remains holding the end of the beard, with the index and middle finger on top, and the bent fourth and little fingers and the thumb on the underside of the beard.*)

K'UANG CHUNG (*takes the register in his left hand, turns to face the prisoners, and reads from the register*): T'ao Fu-chu, Hsiung Yu-lan. (*Holding the book in his left hand, he turns to Hsiung Yu-lan and points to it with his right index and middle fingers outstretched.*) Hsiung Yu-lan, when did you come to Suchou?

HSIUNG YU-LAN (*kneeling upright, head held back in affirmation*): On the eighth day of the fourth month.

K'UANG CHUNG: And when did you leave Ch'angchou?

HSIUNG YU-LAN: The fifteenth day of the fourth month.

K'UANG CHUNG (*to himself*): It really looks as if this Hsiung Yu-lan has been wronged.

SU HSÜ-CHÜAN (*head turned towards the magistrate*): Honored Sir! Now that you have discovered who this gentleman really is, please declare his innocence.

(*K'uang Chung turns towards her, his left hand resting on the table after putting down the register. He gestures towards her with his right middle and index fingers extended.*)

K'UANG CHUNG: Su Hsü-chüan, naturally we can reinvestigate whether you plotted this wicked murder with Hsiung Yu-lan. But when your father was killed, why were you so determined to run away?

SU HSÜ-CHÜAN: Honored Sir, on that evening, when my stepfather returned home he brought fifteen strings of copper cash with him and quite clearly said it was the price for selling me, but because I did not want to be a slave girl, I ran away late at night to take refuge with a relative. How can you say I stole the money and killed my stepfather? What real proof or evidence is there?

(*K'uang Chung turns to face the audience as he speaks to himself. His left hand rests on the desk; his right hand, palm towards him, thumb extended, is raised at chest height.*)

K'UANG CHUNG: If she did not kill him, we must catch the real murderer. If she did not kill him, we must get real proof. How can we grasp at shadows and lightly condemn to death for crime? They must not be executed—they must not be executed! (*He suddenly remembers his own position and his public duty. He rises to his feet.*) Aiya!

(*He sings in the Ch'ien Ch'iang modal pattern.*)

I received orders to supervise the execution.
I have no authority to reverse the decision.
How can I right Ch'angchou wrongs in Suchou Prefecture?

(*As he sings, his left foot is poised forward on the heel. He holds the execution order over the outstretched fingers of his raised left hand, thumb outside, the bottom of the scroll held between the thumb and index finger of the right hand. His head is bent towards the scroll and moves gently up and down as he reads from the order, whose characters are, of course, written in Chinese vertical style.*)

Moreover the Board has already given its order;
How can its command be disobeyed?

(*He puts down the order, holds his right hand vertically in front of him, palm inward, and finally, holds both hands before him, palms upward in a gesture of query. He selects a writing brush with his right hand and pauses.*)

Ah! It cannot be done—it cannot!

(*He stands poised, holding the brush between the thumb and*

*index and third fingers, pointing forward and downwards.
The left hand is raised and placed beneath the right to sup-
port it.*)
This brush is heavy as a thousand catties.[20]
Once used, it signs away two lives.
(*He stands in an air of thoughtfulness, his eyes fixed directly
ahead of him.*)
Since I know injustice has been done,
I must change the decision.
If I mistake the murderer,
How can I count myself an upright official?
(*He lowers his eyes with a movement of decision, his brush
still held poised. Then he calls out firmly.*) Executioners!
Take these prisoners into the anteroom until further orders
are given!
(*The executioners, two standing behind each prisoner, face
each other with outstretched hands, palms uppermost.*)

EXECUTIONER: Begin all over again? Aiya, Your Honor! We received instructions to deal quickly with them; we cannot delay!
(*They turn to face the prefect and go down on their knees in
salutation. The two prisoners raise their heads hopefully.*)

K'UANG CHUNG (*seating himself*): Don't talk so much! I know
what is right!
(*The executioners stand and turn about, two behind each
prisoner, and face each other questioningly. They are about
to seize the prisoners, who now turn to face the audience,
when the third quarter of the second watch sounds from the
drum tower. This is symbolized by drumbeats offstage.*)

EXECUTIONERS: Your Honor, by the fifth watch the prisoners must
be executed. We cannot delay. If we hinder matters any more,
how shall we account for it?
(*The two prisoners turn and lean appealingly towards the prefect, who is sitting with his brush still poised in his hand.*)

K'UANG CHUNG: Ah!
(*He sings.*)
Orders are to execute the prisoners by the fifth watch.

---

20. The Chinese equivalent of a pound equal, in fact, to one and one-
third pounds avoirdupois.

Now it is nearly the third watch.
It will be difficult to reverse the decision,
And I have no plan of action.
My mind is uneasy.
(*Speaking after pausing deep in thought.*) Ah! Since injustice has been done, I am in duty bound to beg for their lives to be saved. (*Turning to the executioners.*) Take the prisoners below!
(*Defeated, the executioners seize the two prisoners and lead them from the court. The prefect, preceded by his assistant, steps down from the dais and goes to center stage. The assistant, facing the audience with his hands held in front of him at waist height, his palms inward, right hand over left, stands to the right of the prefect. The prefect also faces the audience, his left foot placed obliquely in front of his right foot. With his right hand, he grasps the tip of his beard, pulling it over towards his right, and raises his left hand in gesture as he speaks to his assistant.*)
Bring me my ordinary clothes, my seal, and a lantern, and come with me. We're going to the Yamen to get an audience with the governor.

(*Curtain.*)

Scene 5: The Audience with the Governor

The begining of this scene is played in the stage area before the second curtain, which represents the gate of the governor's official residence. K'uang Chung and his assistant enter to the left of the audience.

ASSISTANT: Here we are. (*He turns towards K'uang.*)
K'UANG CHUNG: Right. You wait outside the Yamen for me.
ASSISTANT: Yes, sir. (*He exits right of the audience.*)
K'UANG CHUNG (*standing obliquely to the curtain and facing left of the audience*): Is anyone there?
NIGHT DUTY OFFICER (*offstage*): Who is it? (*He comes on right of the audience.*)

K'UANG CHUNG: It's the prefect K'uang.

NIGHT DUTY OFFICER: So it's you, Your Honor. The execution is over?

K'UANG CHUNG: It's because of the execution that I have come here. I wish to have an audience with the governor: please announce me.

NIGHT DUTY OFFICER: His Excellency has already retired, and it's not convenient to disturb him. Please go back, Your Honor, and come early tomorrow during office hours.

K'UANG CHUNG: I have urgent business that cannot wait!

NIGHT DUTY OFFICER: Your humble servant, but I have to think of my career. I dare not announce you!

K'UANG CHUNG: Supposing you are interfering with important business, are you willing to take responsibility?

(*The prefect is standing with his left hand holding his jade girdle and his right hand holding the extremity of the right strip of his beard between his thumb, index, and middle fingers. His head is turned towards the officer; his expression is stern. The officer backs away, right arm held across his waist, fingers extended palm inwards, and parallel with his left arm, which is extended forward towards the prefect.*)

NIGHT DUTY OFFICER: This . . . er . . . Your Honor is not like other officials. Wait and your humble servant will go and announce you. (*He exits right of the audience.*)

K'UANG CHUNG: Heh! That fellow hasn't the courage of a mouse! (*The night duty officer reenters.*)

NIGHT DUTY OFFICER: Your Honor!

K'UANG CHUNG: Well?

NIGHT DUTY OFFICER: Your humble servant went to announce you. His Excellency was exceedingly annoyed. Only the mention of Your Honor's name saved me from being punished. He sent a message to ask Your Honor to come back tomorrow and see him in his office.

K'UANG CHUNG (*standing in the same position as before*): This is a matter of life and death: how can you say wait until tomorrow? Go and announce me again!

NIGHT DUTY OFFICER (*backing away fearfully once again, his hands as previously described*): Your humble servant must think of his own neck! (*He hurriedly exits.*)

K'UANG CHUNG: Aiya! What's the best thing to do? (*He turns to stare at the drum, which is placed at the right of the stage to the audience; it represents the official drum of the governor's quarters, which is beaten in times of emergency only. He seizes the drumstick, which has been suspended on its support, and stands holding it vertically in his right hand at head height. He is grasping his right water sleeve lightly with his left hand. His head is turned to his left, and he is looking upwards with eyes fixed in a stare.*) There's nothing for it; I must beat the drum!

(*He relaxes his pose and beats the drum twice. A voice is heard giving orders offstage.*)

VOICE OFF: The governor has issued a command and wants to know what stupid idiot is making all that din on the Court drum. If he has an official plea, first give him forty strokes before his case is heard. If he has no plea, give him a severe beating double the number of strokes and tell him to get out! (*Guards are heard to respond to this order. The captain of the guard enters the stage right of the audience and stands, left leg thrust forward, left hand held outstretched towards the prefect; his right arm is bent and raised at waist height, the hand grasping one end of the sash which hangs down beneath his jacket.*)

CAPTAIN OF THE GUARD (*threateningly*): Who beat the drum?

K'UANG CHUNG (*turning towards the captain, hands on his jade girdle, right foot forward and at right angles to the left, left foot in the rear*): I did! Moreover, I have no official plea, so what's to be done?

CAPTAIN OF THE GUARD: Your Honor must be joking! Wait; your humble servant will go and announce you to the governor!

K'UANG CHUNG: Thank you for your trouble. (*He turns to the audience as the captain exits right of the audience.*) A fox playing the tiger! How disgusting!

VOICE OFF: Your Honor is invited to an audience! Your Honor is invited to an audience!

(*The captain returns.*)

CAPTAIN OF THE GUARD: His Excellency the Governor invites Your Honor to an audience.

K'UANG CHUNG: Thank you for your trouble.
  (*The two men go off to the right of the audience.*)

  (*The second curtain is now drawn and looped back on either side to reveal the governor's audience chamber in the third acting area. In the rear center of this area of the stage is the governor's dais, on which his chair stands in front of an ornate, scenic canopy with side pieces. In the second acting area at the point where the second curtain is looped back, right of the audience, stands a high, ornate, metal candle holder. In front of this are two plain, short-backed, wooden chairs on either side of a plain, rectangular table, which stands as high as the backs of the chairs and separates them. The furnishings are covered with crimson-embroidered silk coverings. K'uang Chung comes on, led by the captain of the guard.*)

CAPTAIN OF THE GUARD: Please wait a minute.
  (*He exits right of the audience. K'uang Chung turns to face the audience chamber and then walks over to seat himself on one of the chairs just described. He sits with both hands grasping his jade girdle on either side. After a few moments, he gives signs of impatience. He thrusts his left foot forward so that it is poised on the heel. He then raises both hands, palms upwards, water sleeves hanging over wrists, and shakes them in an attitude of despair. The captain comes on again, and K'uang Chung stands, thinking the governor is arriving; but the captain goes off and the prefect sits down despairingly again. The last quarter before the fourth watch sounds. The captain's voice is heard offstage.*)

CAPTAIN OF THE GUARD: Listen! His Excellency has ordered the guards to escort him to the audience chamber.
  (*K'uang gets to his feet, shakes his hands, palms upturned, and then stands leaning towards the audience chamber in the third acting area as though listening. His feet are apart, his left hand is on the jade girdle, and his right hand is raised at chest height in front of him, palm down, fingers outstretched. Nothing .happens, and he straightens up, and in turn, kicks each leg forward and upward to waist height, with a broad movement which reveals the sole of his boot to the audience. As each leg is raised, the opposite arm is raised to*)

*shoulder height, the water sleeves flung loose, and then
grasped at the apex of the movement. He then bends his head,
water sleeves in position again, holding his hands in front of
him with right-hand fingers lightly placed over the left and
facing the side of the stage left of the audience.*)

K'UANG CHUNG (*recites*):

Anxious in heart . . .

(*He turns to face the audience, his arms held wide in appeal
towards them.*)

I can neither stand nor sit.

Time is limited

If I am to save them from the executioner's sword.

(*He lifts his right hand in front of his face, palm facing left,
thumb extended; his left arm is bent outward, his left foot
forward and. poised on the heel. He sings in the Shih Liu
Hua modal pattern.*)

I never thought he would be as hard as stone,

(*He bends forward, his upturned palms lifted at chest height,
and his right foot lifted high.*)

As immovable as Mount T'ai.[21]

(*He lifts both hands to shoulder height, palms outward, little
fingers slightly apart from the others, thumbs bent forward.*)

The patient's condition is critical, yet the doctor delays.

(*He turns left slightly, arms a little lower, index and middle
fingers of both hands extended, left foot placed forward and
poised on the heel.*)

Each beat of the watch drum troubles my mind.

Now I know why they say

Passing time is ten thousand times more precious than gold.

(*He places his feet apart, bends slightly towards his right,
and raises his hands, palms upturned, the extremity of his
beard resting on his right palm.*)

To enter the Yamen to see a high official

Is as difficult as diving to the bottom of the sea.

(*He faces to his left, left foot forward, and flings both arms*

---

21. Mount T'ai, in western Shantung, was regarded as sacred by the
Chinese and figured in countless proverbs. It was the most famous of five
sacred mountains, the other four being situated in Hunan, Shensi, Hopei,
and Honan provinces.

*downwards by his side so that the water sleeves hang fully
extended to touch the floor.*

*Four guards now appear on stage, followed by the captain
of the guard, and range themselves at the right of the governor's audience chamber. After an interval the governor
Chou Ch'en, appears and walks to center stage. The governor takes up a position in front of his ranged retinue, who
bow from the waist; and with head erect, he sweeps his beard
from top to bottom with both hands, the thumbs beneath, the
extended fingers uppermost. He then seats himself on the
dais in the way described for other officials. The captain of
the guard stands behind him. K'uang Chung walks over to
the center stage to face the governor. As he bows, K'uang
thrusts his left foot forward poised on the heel, raises his
hands in front of him, right clasped over the left, and bends
his head deeply above them.)*

K'UANG CHUNG: Your Excellency!

CHOU CH'EN: Please sit down.

K'UANG CHUNG: Thank you. (*He returns to his seat and sits facing
the governor, his feet wide apart, hands raised at waist height
before him.*)

CHOU CH'EN: We received a sentence of execution by Imperial
Decree. We have already asked that Your Honor assist by
presiding over the execution in accordance with the law. For
what reason do you come here by night and beat the drum?

K'UANG CHUNG: Because the two prisoners have not yet been
proved guilty, Your Excellency. So I came here tonight to
beg for a postponement until we find out the truth.

CHOU CH'EN: Why do you say they are not proved guilty?

K'UANG CHUNG: Although Su Hsü-chüan was travelling with
Hsiung Yu-lan and although he was carrying the identical
amount of money stolen from Yu Hu-lu, yet I found many
discrepancies when I examined the case. We are not justified
in assuming that they were lovers who murdered the old man.
Your Excellency!

(*He rises to his feet and begins to sing in the Wei Fan Hsu
modal pattern. He steps forward a pace with each line, one
foot forward, heel poised, hands emphasizing the words with
gesture.*)

How can they be declared guilty just for travelling together?
(*He is bent slightly forward, left leg thrust out, poised on the heel, hands at chest height, palms inward, thumbs extended, right hand above the left.*)
The money by itself is not evidence.
This case is doubtful.
We must make another careful investigation.

CHOU CH'EN (*raising his right hand and sweeping the right strand of his beard downwards with his index and middle fingers, the thumb on the underside of the beard*): Three trials and six cross-examinations—think how many courts this case has already been through. It is already closed. Your Honor need trouble himself with it no further.

K'UANG CHUNG: Your Excellency, do not say that!
(*He sings once more. His hands are raised in front of him, palms down, fingers spread apart; his left foot is forward and poised on the heel.*)
How can we so lightly pass sentence of death,
Destroying innocent people
To become wronged ghosts?

CHOU CH'EN (*raising his left arm before him*): The magistrate of Wuhsi and the prefect of Ch'angchou are officials appointed by the Emperor and good servants of the State; they have great experience and are well versed in affairs; they cannot have been mistaken in this case. Moreover, I gave the final verdict: if there had been injustice, I would have put it right. Your Honor should not worry about these matters.

K'UANG CHUNG (*moving nearer to the governor, who sits with head averted, hands on his jade girdle*): As Your Excellency passed the final verdict, may I know if Hsiung Yu-lan is really the employee of the merchant T'ao Fu-chu and where the fifteen strings of cash really came from? Since Hsiung Yu-lan's home is in Huaian and Su Hsü-chüan lives at Wuhsi, how did they get to know each other? Who can prove these two were lovers?
(*He strides away from the dais and half faces the audience. His left hand is raised, index finger extended, little finger curved above the rest, and he holds his beard to one side with his right hand.*) According to what I have found by

sending someone to the Yüeh-lai Inn opposite the Taoist temple——

CHOU CH'EN (*interrupting with his right hand raised before him at face height and then lowered again parallel with the left hand at chest height*): Stop! I am responsible for many districts south of the Yangtze, and there are state affairs I cannot deal with in person. How can you expect me to investigate a paltry case like this? I had the Ch'angchou papers to confirm matters. How can you call this a trumped-up charge?

(*K'uang Chung has turned towards the governor to listen to his protest, and stands with his left foot placed forward and poised on the heel. His right hand is held at waist height; his extended left-hand fingers are held before his mouth, and he strokes his beard. He then turns away and walks towards his seat, his hands held forward, palms downwards, as he speaks*).

K'UANG CHUNG: But the lives of men are not to be treated like playthings. This case requires closer investigation, in my opinion.

(*He sings.*)

Proof, we must have real proof.
We cannot decide on empty words.

(*He turns to face the governor, who holds up his left hand while looking haughtily to his right.*)

CHOU CH'EN: Your honor, there is one point I do not understand. Please explain it to me.

K'UANG CHUNG: What is it you do not understand?

CHOU CH'EN: What is the duty of an official supervising an execution?

K'UANG CHUNG: To verify the criminal, have him executed promptly, and make his report.

CHOU CH'EN: When something is not his concern?

K'UANG CHUNG: Then he should not try to interfere.

CHOU CH'EN: I asked you to supervise this execution. You should simply perform your task. Why did you leave your post, exceeding your duty and meddling in other's affairs?

(*The governor has stepped down from his dais and goes towards K'uang Chung, his right hand on his jade girdle, his left arm raised towards the prefect, palm upwards, fingers closed. K'uang Chung stands to the governor's left, hands held before him at chest height, head inclined slightly to his left, eyes fixed on the governor to the right.*)

K'UANG CHUNG: Your Excellency, the law permits us to listen to condemned people who cry out that they have been wronged and to reconsider their cases. I only ask Your Excellency to order innocent lives to be saved.

CHOU CH'EN: The order has already come from the Ministry. What can I do?

(*The governor faces the audience, arms extended in front of him, the palms of his hands uppermost and partially covered by the long water sleeves hanging from the wrists. He sings in the Ch'ien Ch'iang modal pattern.*)

You only cause needless difficulty.
The law of the land is like a rock.
I am only a small official:
I cannot act irregularly.

(*His head inclined to the left, his right hand held forward and raised vertically, fingers apart and extended, thumb bent, K'uang Chung leans towards the governor. K'uang's left hand is placed on his jade girdle at his left side. His right foot is forward and poised on the heel.*)

K'UANG CHUNG: As officials, we are responsible to the State above and the people below. I find it hard to treat men's lives as of no account in this way.

(*The fourth watch sounds from the drum tower.*)

CHOU CH'EN: Your Honor!

(*He sings again, moving forward past the prefect to take up his position front stage. His head is raised, with his glance directed upward; his left hand is raised to face height, index finger extended, and his right hand is held at chest height.*)

Listen to the drum tower:
Time is passing.
I expect Your Honor
To hurry back;
If we interfere with the hour of execution,
It will be difficult for both of us.

K'UANG CHUNG (*standing in the background, facing left of the stage to the audience, head lowered, hands raised before him*): Your Excellency . . .

(*He turns to walk towards the governor, who also turns to*

face the prefect. The governor's right hand is extended, his left arm held at waist height.)

CHOU CH'EN: What!

(*With his left foot thrust forward and poised on the heel, his right hand over the left in front of him, and his head bowed respectfully, K'uang Chung stands before the governor. The governor has raised his right hand to face height.*)

K'UANG CHUNG (*sings*):
The ruler is no more precious than the people.
If ordinary people are wrongly accused,
An official must be ashamed at heart
Not to help them.
I willingly face instant dismissal from office!
(*He is turned away from the governor and looks over his right shoulder. Both hands are extended to the left, the right arm bent across his chest to make a line with the extended left arm; the fingers are extended, palms downward and thumbs wide apart. His right foot is placed well forward; his left foot is well in the rear and placed at right angles to the right foot.*)

CHOU CH'EN: This is a grave matter; it is difficult for me to interfere. Think no more about it, Your Honor.
(*He has walked across the stage behind the prefect and stands facing his dais, with his back to the audience. K'uang Chung turns towards him, places his hands together, and makes a deep obeisance, his left leg extended sideways and poised on the heel.*)

K'UANG CHUNG: If Your Excellency fears the consequences, you can transfer full responsibility to me.
(*He straightens up and begins to sing. The governor has turned to face him.*)
This humble person has received the Imperial Mandate
To do what I think is necessary after due deliberation.
If my subordinates do not govern well,
I have power to arrest and try them.
If I meet injustice, how can I disregard it?

CHOU CH'EN: Hm, hm!

K'UANG CHUNG (*singing*):
Your Excellency,
I beg you to give your gracious permission!

CHOU CH'EN (*angrily, his hands held before him at chest height*):

Since you intend to take matters into your own hands, why do you bother to ask me?

(*He sings in the Ch'ien Ch'iang modal pattern.*)

Since you have the Emperor's mandate

To do as you please,

Why did you bother to come here in the first place?

As for me, my whole life I have been careful

Never to commit a breach of the rules.

(*The governor turns angrily away to his left, his hands holding up the jade girdle around his waist. The prefect stands with left foot thrust forward and poised on the heel. The thumb and index finger of his left hand grasp the right water sleeve, which covers the right hand. He has an expression of triumph on his face.*)

K'UANG CHUNG: Your Excellency, please do not be angry. This humble person only wishes to help the people!

CHOU CH'EN: On no account will I go back on my order!

K'UANG CHUNG: Ah, since Your Excellency refuses, I will leave my gold seal here as guarantee and ask for your clemency in granting me a few months to go to Wuhsi and Ch'angchou to investigate the affair in person. I will make a report on my return. Please grant your permission. (*He is facing the audience as he speaks, his heels together and his feet at an angle of forty-five degrees. He raises his right arm before him, and from inside the sleeve, he takes his gold seal with his left hand.*)

CHOU CH'EN (*laughs coldly and turns towards him, right hand raised at face height, left hand by his side*)· It is so rare to find a prefect with such concern for his people that it is difficult to refuse. Keep your seal. I give you permission to go. (*K'uang Chung is standing with his left arm raised across his chest, the thumb, forefinger, and middle finger grasping the right water sleeve, while the right hand holds out the seal towards the governor. The two men turn to face each other, the prefect still with his seal held before him, his left foot extended sideways and poised on the heel.*)

K'UANG CHUNG: Many thanks, Your Excellency. May I have the arrow of command?[22]

---

22. The arrow of command was originally a small, triangular pennant attached and bestowed by the Emperor as a symbol of vested authority.

CHOU CH'EN: What do you want with the arrow of command?

K'UANG CHUNG: Ch'angchou and Wuhsi are not under my humble jurisdiction. I shall be able to do my work better if I have Your Excellency's authority.

(*The governor turns, and with his back to the audience, goes to his official seat. K'uang Chung turns to face the audience, left foot forward, hands held in front of him and apart; he holds his seal in his left hand.*)

CHOU CH'EN (*from his seat*): Bring the arrow of command here!

(*K'uang Chung turns to face the governor and makes his deep obeisance, his left foot forward. The captain of the guard steps down from the dais, bows before the governor, then turns to hand K'uang Chung the arrow of command. The captain's right foot is thrust forward at a right angle to the left; both arms are outstretched at shoulder height, the right hand proffering the arrow of command. K'uang Chung turns to take it and then stands posed, holding it in front of him, his eyes lowered on the treasured symbol of authority. With his left hand he lifts the lower front portion of his robe to his waist, revealing his crimson silk trousers. His left leg is thrust forward. The whole pose is symbolic of achieving his end.*)

K'UANG CHUNG: Many thanks, Your Excellency! (*He turns to leave.*)

CHOU CH'EN: A moment, Your Honor! (*He steps down from the dais again and walks to center stage to face the prefect.*) Before you go, remember that you have a time limit of two weeks!

(*K'uang Chung stands speechless. His left hands holds the arrow of command, which is supported in the crook of his raised left elbow, the stem of the arrow being held between the extended index and middle fingers. His right hand grasps his robe just below the jade girdle at the right, drawing the front portion of the garment above and to the right of his feet, which are placed squarely together. The governor next*

On the traditional Chinese stage it is a small property used frequently to symbolize the granting of special authority or command. So used, it is a small, wooden baton with a broad, pointed end, tapering away into a short grip at the other extremity.

*turns to face the audience, his hands lifted in emphasis to
K'uang Chung, who has also turned to face the audience.
K'uang holds his right hand pensively before his beard at
the level of his mouth; his left hand still supports the arrow
of command, and his feet are placed squarely together. The
governor continues angrily.)*
If you are not able to get to the bottom of this affair in two
weeks, I shall report it to the Emperor! Ha, ha! Do not expect
any sympathy then!
*(He flicks his right water sleeve brusquely downwards, re-
places it in position, then angrily stalks past K'uang Chung
and makes his exit to the right of the audience, followed by
the captain of the guard and the guards. K'uang Chung stands
facing the audience, feet together, staring fixedly at the arrow
of command, now held vertically before him in his right hand
while his left hand grasps the bottom of his beard, which is
drawn over to the left. Then, with a quick movement, he
drops his hand from his beard and pulls back the lower front
portion of his robe to reveal his crimson trousers once again.
Posing in this way, he makes a sharp turn to his right, right
foot first, and strides offstage to the left of the audience.)*
(Curtain.)

Scene 6: The Rat is Suspected

*The scene begins before the drawn second curtain, the stage
area representing a street setting. The local district headman enters
left of the audience.*

HEADMAN *(reciting as he moves to center stage)*:
    Who would be a headman?
    Kept busy day and night, it's never-ending night and day,
    Now someone's coming to reinvestigate a murder case.
    In and out, out and in, always on the trot:
    There's no peace.[23]

23. The Chinese original is a neat, alliterative rhyme in a four-line
stanza:

(*Calling out.*) Neighbors, please all gather here!
(*The neighbors of the first scene file onto the stage, one after the other, the last in line being Lou the Rat. They stand in a row looking at the headman, who stands facing the audience, left hand akimbo, right hand raised in explanation as he turns his head towards them.*)

NEIGHBORS: What is it you want?

HEADMAN: It's Yu Hu-lu's murder case. The Suchou prefect K'uang will be here shortly to make an investigation. I want you all to wait for him and answer his questions afterwards.

NEIGHBOR A: If he's the Suchou prefect, how can he deal with a Ch'angchou case?

HEADMAN: Prefect K'uang has the arrow of command from the governor.

NEIGHBOR A: But the real criminals have already been caught. Why does he want to make another investigation?

NEIGHBORS (*in unison*): Yes, why?

HEADMAN: Prefect K'uang is a sincere official; he says an injustice has been done. Neighbors, please follow me.
(*All exit in a file after the headman, except Lou the Rat, who remains center stage looking thoughtful and extremely agitated. He stands facing the audience, his feet a little apart and his knees bent. He is stroking his chin with his right hand, which he lowers, palm uppermost, and uses to emphasize points of the soliloquy that follows.*)

LOU THE RAT: Aiya! I thought Hsiung Yu-lan and Su Hsü-chüan were unhappy ghosts by now. How is it that Prefect K'uang is coming to reinvestigate the case? Can they suspect that I, Lou the Rat, am involved? (*He turns his body sharply to his left, as though frightened at the thought, and leans forward on his left leg, his right leg stretched to the full, the foot pointing to the front. His hands are clasped together in front of his waist, and he looks down at the floor.*) No, no, that's impossible! In the first place, nobody saw me do the deed, so nobody can know. There are no witnesses and no evidence,

> Wei jen ch'ieh mo tso ti fang
> Jih, jih, yeh, yeh, pan po mang
> Jo shih ch'u la jen ming an
> Li, li, wai, wai, p'ao tuan ch'ang.

so what is there to fear? I'll mix in with the neighbors and pretend to be an honest fellow, trim my sails to the prevailing wind, and do as occasion demands. (*He turns towards the audience again, left foot forward; with his left hand he rubs the back of his neck as he looks downwards to his right. His movements are quick and furtive: indeed, there is something ratlike in his gestures, and the skillful comic actor makes great play with such qualities.*) Aiya! It can't be done, it can't be done! That K'uang Chung is known as a second Pao Ch'eng, wise and full of strategy—a terrible man to be up against. If I give the game away and he realizes it, it will be too late to escape. The proverb has it: "Of the thirty-six strategies, the best plan is to flee." Wait—I'll go and hide in the country for ten days or so and come back later when this affair's blown over. I'll take myself off.

(*He goes off to the left of the audience, looking back fearfully over his left shoulder, his knees lifted high, arms bent at waist level, and his hands with fingers clenched turned down from the wrists, rather like paws. He creeps furtively away with quickening pace.*)

(*Two court runners enter to the left of the audience. They are followed, in turn, by K'uang Chung's assistant, the district magistrate Kuo Yü-chih, and the Suchou prefect K'uang Chung. The group goes to center stage; the court runners and K'uang's assistant stand in the rear. Kuo faces the audience, his right hand lifted in front of him at chest height and his left holding his jade girdle. K'uang Chung is a little behind him to his left.*)

K'UANG CHUNG: I do not fear troubling myself for the people.

KUO YÜ-CHIH: I dread these impractical people.

(*The headman comes on left of the audience and goes up to the group.*)

HEADMAN: Welcome, Your Honors; I bow before you. (*He goes down on his knees, head bent and hands clasped before him.*)

K'UANG CHUNG: Get up. Where is Yu Hu-lu's house?

HEADMAN (*rising and indicating the curtain*): Just in front of us.

K'UANG CHUNG: Lead the way.

HEADMAN: Yes, sir!

(*The curtain rises to show them standing before the setting of the first scene, the interior of Yu Hu-lu's house and shop.*)

K'UANG CHUNG: Open the door.

HEADMAN: Yes, sir! (*He goes through the pantomime of breaking the seals fixed by the Court, shooting the bolts, and opening door.*)

K'UANG CHUNG (*bowing to Kuo Yü-chih*): Please go in.

KUO YÜ-CHIH: Your Honor first.

K'UANG CHUNG: Let's enter together.

(*They step over the threshold together and find the house thick with dust, which is expressed by the magistrates' flinging their long water sleeves out and flicking them right and left in long sweeps. The group finally takes up a position with Kuo Yü-chih standing in front of the dead pork butcher's bench facing the audience, K'uang Chung to his left, the assistant to K'uang's left, and the two court runners on either side of K'uang to his rear. The headman is at center stage facing this group. Kuo Yü-chih places his right foot forward, his left hand supporting his jade girdle, and gestures to K'uang Chung with his right hand.*)

KUO YÜ-CHIH: Please begin your investigations, Your Honor.

K'UANG CHUNG: Let us do it together. Headman!

HEADMAN (*placing his left foot forward*): Here, sir!

K'UANG CHUNG (*both hands extended at waist height before him*): Where was Yu Hu-lu killed?

HEADMAN (*pointing to the spot on the floor in front of him*): He died here.

K'UANG CHUNG: Where did you find the weapon?

HEADMAN (*pointing*): We found it here.

K'UANG CHUNG: When did you hold the inquest and bury him?

HEADMAN: Three days after he was killed.

K'UANG CHUNG: And the weapon?

HEADMAN: It was taken to the court as evidence in the case.

(*His left hand supporting his jade girdle, K'uang Chung turns to Kuo Yü-chih. K'uang holds a folded fan, which he has taken from his collar, in his right hand, with the bottom end of the fan between the thumb, first, and middle fingers, the fourth and little fingers extended. Kuo also holds a fan, but horizontally in his right hand, which is partially hidden by his water sleeve. His left hand, also partially covered by his sleeve, is extended, palm uppermost, towards K'uang. The senior magistrate is leaning forward and looking up at K'uang Chung with an air of impatience.*)

K'UANG CHUNG: Did you yourself investigate the case at the time, Your Honor?

KUO YÜ-CHIH: Since the murderers had already been caught, why should I have raised the matter again?

(*K'uang Chung turns away and begins to examine the door, testing the knocker and scrutinizing all parts. There is no actual door, of course, and the actions are pantomimed. Finding nothing suspicious, he goes to the chopping block, leans over, and tests the wooden wall behind the block. He then mimes sliding aside a panel opening out of the shop. A cloud of dust arises, and everyone steps back, simulating brushing it away with their sleeves and dusting their clothing. K'uang Chung next examines the bed and the wall. Finally, he looks intently at the bloodstains on the floor; as he straightens up, Kuo Yü-chih bends with exaggerated posture to stare at them also.*)

KUO YÜ-CHIH (*with mock surprise*): Ah, those are bloodstains!

K'UANG CHUNG: Yes, bloodstains.

KUO YÜ-CHIH: I fear they are those of the murdered man.

K'UANG CHUNG: Naturally. They cannot be the murderer's.

KUO YÜ-CHIH: Those bloodstains have a close connection with the murder; we must examine them most carefully.

K'UANG CHUNG: Naturally, we should examine them carefully.

(*As they talk, the two men are facing the audience. Kuo's head is inclined a little to the right; he holds his closed fan upright in his right hand and emphasizes his points with it. K'uang stands holding his closed fan in front of him as described previously. His left hand, palm uppermost and fingers open, is held before him at chest height.*)

KUO YÜ-CHIH: Aiya! No matter how much you look at them, you still do not know who the murderer is.

K'UANG CHUNG: What is Your Honor's opinion?

KUO YÜ-CHIH (*laughs ironically*): My opinion?

K'UANG CHUNG: Who did it?

KUO YÜ-CHIH: But Your Honor says they have been unjustly sentenced.

K'UANG CHUNG (*to the headman*): Where is Su Hsü-chüan's room?
HEADMAN: Just inside there.
K'UANG CHUNG: What was she like?
HEADMAN: Quiet and reserved in manner.
KUO YÜ-CHIH (*interrupting*): When an unmarried girl has a lover, naturally she pretends to be quiet and reserved in manner to deceive others!
(*K'uang Chung gives Kuo a scornful glance and goes into the inner room, i.e., he disappears behind the set representing the bed at the left of the stage to the audience. Kuo Yü-chih laughs sarcastically and steps forward to face the audience, his hands held before him at waist height and his fan in his left hand. He finishes by turning to his right and opening the fan with both hands before he sings.*)
KUO YÜ-CHIH (*singing in the T'ai Shih Tin modal pattern*):
She is really guilty, but he insists she is innocent;
There is plenty of evidence, yet he wants to make new inquiries,
Trying to treat murderers as law-abiding citizens.
It's laughable! How absurd! What a fool he is!
(*Kuo has flicked his fan shut with a single movement very shortly after beginning to sing. Now he reopens the fan with a flourish just as K'uang Chung reenters. The others in the group have remained standing in the background the whole time this action has been going on. Kuo Yü-chih turns to face K'uang Chung, who stands before the bed, feet placed together, hands held extended forward at chest height.*)
Has Your Honor been able to find anything suspicious?
K'UANG CHUNG: Have you?
KUO YÜ-CHIH (*gazing intently at the ground*): Ah! Everything is suspicious!
(*The two men move closer together; each has his closed fan in his right hand to emphasize his words in gesture.*)
K'UANG CHUNG: What is suspicious and why?
KUO YÜ-CHIH: If there is nothing suspicious, why has Your Honor come to make an investigation?
K'UANG CHUNG: You mean that I should mind my own affairs.
KUO YÜ-CHIH: Oh, no, I would not say such a thing. Your Honor looks after the people! (*He opens his arms widely in front of*

*him at waist height, his fan pointing forward in his right
hand, his head held erect, and a cynical smile on his face.*)

K'UANG CHUNG: And what about Your Honor?

KUO YÜ-CHIH (*bows deeply, both hands holding the closed fan
stretched horizontally in front of him*): As for my humble
self, I am ignorant. I examined the case according to the evidence and made my verdict, but if Your Honor says I
blundered, he must know better than the others.

(*Sings.*)

Your Honor is talented and full of wisdom.

Once you have investigated the case,

You will certainly know everything!

K'UANG CHUNG: I only fear I shall find nothing, and come and
go after laboring in vain.

KUO YÜ-CHIH: Your Honor has an idea in mind. How can you
come and go, laboring in vain? (*Laughing.*) Please go on
with your search.

K'UANG CHUNG: I will! (*He walks towards the butcher's chopping
block and suddenly stops. His feet are placed wide apart at
an angle, his knees bent, and his eyes fixed on the floor. His
right arm is thrust behind his back; and his left arm is bent
across his chest, the palm of the hand downwards and the
first and little fingers raised higher than the rest. He bends to
pick up a coin.*) Ah! Here is a copper coin on the floor.

(*One of the court runners stoops suddenly.*)

RUNNER: Here is another coin!

(*He is down on his left knee in front of K'uang, who, from
the position described previously, leans over and seizes the
coin in his left hand, his right hand still behind his back,
from the runner. K'uang straightens up to look at the coins,
one held in each hand. Kuo Yü-chih has turned his back on
K'uang and stands facing left of the stage to the audience.*)

KUO YÜ-CHIH: What do you expect to find out from those two
coins?

K'UANG CHUNG: Make another search!

(*Everyone looks around, and one of the court runners
searches at the back of the bed.*)

RUNNER: Your Honor, there's more than half a string of cash behind the bed here!

(K'uang Chung strides over quickly to look at the runner's find.)

K'UANG CHUNG *(stands pondering)*: Strange for this half string of cash to be here.

(Kuo Yü-chih walks over to K'uang and points with his fan to the floor, as K'uang remains standing with hands extended before him, his fan held closed in his right hand.)

KUO YÜ-CHIH: Your Honor, Yu Hu-lu was a butcher. He may have dropped the cash in error. There's nothing strange about that.

K'UANG CHUNG: Call the neighbors in!

HEADMAN *(calls out)*: Neighbors, come here!

(Kuo Yü-chih turns towards the audience holding his fan at either end with each hand so that it is horizontally placed across his chest. His head is held high in contempt.)

KUO YÜ-CHIH: The neighbors were all witnesses in the case, and they all approved my verdict. Whether you question them or not makes no difference.

(The neighbors all troop in at the right of the stage and form a group roughly in the shape of a V, with the headman at the apex near the bed, and next to him on his right, K'uang's assistant. The assistant has placed a chair for his master, who now sits with his legs stretched out, feet wide apart, and left hand supporting his jade girdle, ready for his cross examination. Kuo Yü-chih is standing a little distance from K'uang, still holding his fan with both hands. He faces the audience, right foot forward, as though disinterested in the proceedings. The neighbors move forward a little towards K'uang and bow.)

NEIGHBORS *(in unison)*: We bow before Your Honor!

K'UANG CHUNG: Stand up. What state were Yu Hu-lu's affairs in?

CH'IN KU-HSIN *(stepping forward a little and emphasizing his words with his right hand, which is half hidden by his water sleeve)*: Yu Hu-lu had been out of business for some time and lived by borrowing and pawning.

THE OTHER NEIGHBORS *(in unison)*: His household never knew where their next meal was coming from!

K'UANG CHUNG: Ah!

(He sings.)

If Yu Hu-lu's houeshold had not enough to eat,
Why was this money dropped on the floor?

KUO YÜ-CHIH (*turning towards K'uang*): Yu Hu-lu was a drunkard and a muddleheaded fool. He must have left the money before he went out of business and forgotten about it.

K'UANG CHUNG: Ah!

(*He sings.*)

He might forget a few coins,
But half a string of cash would be difficult!

(*The neighbors glance at the money and talk among themselves in two small groups between the bed and the butcher's chopping block.*)

KUO YÜ-CHIH: Where does Your Honor think the half string of cash has come from, then?

K'UANG CHUNG: That's what I'm wondering too. Where does the half string of cash come from?

CH'IN KU-HSIN (*turning to the prefect*): May I humbly suggest that this half string of cash belongs to those fifteen strings of cash.

NEIGHBOR A: Why should half a string fall off?

NEIGHBOR B: Perhaps the murderer was in such a hurry to get away that he dropped it!

NEIGHBOR A: But there wasn't a coin missing from the fifteen strings carried by the murderer.

NEIGHBORS C AND D: Perhaps the man they arrested wasn't the real murderer at all.

CH'IN KU-HSIN: Probably that Hsiung Yu-lan——

(*Kuo Yü-chih gives a great snort, and Ch'in is too scared to continue.*)

KUO YÜ-CHIH: Probably Hsiung Yu-lan did not know there was money behind the bed, or he'd have taken that too!

K'UANG CHUNG (*to the first court runner*): Take that money as further evidence in the case!

FIRST RUNNER: Yes, sir! (*As he goes to pick up the money behind the bed, the runner finds a tiny, square wooden box.*) Your Honor! I've just found a small wooden box.

K'UANG CHUNG: Bring it here!

(*The runner comes forward and goes down on his left knee*

before K'uang Chung, who leans forward to take the box in both hands and then stands up.)
There's a pair of dice inside. Why do they feel so heavy?
(*He stands facing the audience, feet together, holding the dice box before him in his right hand. His assistant stands to his left holding the arrow of command poised in his crooked left arm. The two court runners are at his right, craning forward to see the dice box. The rest of the group stand peering in the background and talking among themselves. Kuo Yü-chih is at the extreme left of K'uang and the runners.*)

FIRST RUNNER: Perhaps they are weighted with lead!

K'UANG CHUNG: Yes, I think they are!

KUO YÜ-CHIH: There's nothing strange about that: the people here have an evil reputation, and every house has dice like those.

K'UANG CHUNG (*stepping forward*): Your Honor!
(*He sings in the Ch'ien Ch'iang modal pattern.*)
These dice are loaded;
That is not very common.
They must belong to a gambler and a cheat.
(*The two men are now front stage. K'uang stands with arms widely extended at chest height before him. Kuo Yü-chih faces him at his right, his fan in his right hand, body slightly bent towards K'uang, who stands upright with feet squarely together.*)

KUO YÜ-CHIH: Since Yu Hu-lu drank heavily, he liked to gamble. Those dice are certainly his.

K'UANG CHUNG (*turning left to face the neighbors*): Tell me, neighbors, was Yu Hu-lu fond of gambling? (*His water sleeves hang in position from the wrists; his left arm is extended at waist height; his fan, held in the right hand, is directed at Ch'in Ku-hsin across the top of his left water sleeve.*)

NEIGHBORS (*in unison*): He drank heavily but never gambled!

KUO YÜ-CHIH: Then some of his close friends dropped them there.
(*Kuo, to the right of K'uang Chung, points with his fan to the floor.*)

K'UANG CHUNG (*appeals to the neighbors with hands outstretched, palms uppermost*): Did any of his close friends gamble?

NEIGHBORS (*in unison*): We knew all his close friends. There was no gambler among them!

K'UANG CHUNG: Please leave us for a while, neighbors.

(*They all file off to the right of the audience, only the headman remaining behind.*)

Headman, any gamblers among these neighbors?

KUO YÜ-CHIH: Of course there are!

HEADMAN: There's not a single gambler among the neighbors!

K'UANG CHUNG: Besides them, is there anybody else?

KUO YÜ-CHIH: He's already said there's no gambler.

HEADMAN: Yes, there's one.

K'UANG CHUNG: What is his name?

HEADMAN: He's called Lou the Rat.

K'UANG CHUNG: Did he often come to see Yu Hu-lu?

KUO YÜ-CHIH: Of course he came often. If he didn't come here, how could he have dropped his dice here?

HEADMAN: Because he often took Yu Hu-lu's pork without paying for it, the two ordinarily never met.

(*Kuo Yü-chih faces K'uang with his right hand uplifted, palm outwards. K'uang standing half turned towards Kuo, holds his bent left arm at chest height, palm upwards; his right hand is raised vertically from the wrist, a little higher than the left hand, with the first and little fingers extended, the thumb and middle finger touching. K'uang's assistant stands facing him directly to the left, his hands on his hips; the two court runners stand in the background on either side of the headman.*)

KUO YÜ-CHIH (*sings in the Liu P'o Mao modal pattern*):
Your Honor, many a thorough investigation like this
Is a waste of effort.
Proof of this kind is never-ending.

K'UANG CHUNG (*singing in the Ch'ien Ch'iang modal pattern*):
I shall continue to make a thorough investigation
And spare no effort.
(*Speaks.*) If Your Honor is busy and does not wish to continue the investigation,
(*Sings.*)
Please return to your office.

It does not matter: I will carry on alone.
(*K'uang Chung has placed his left hand on his jade girdle. His right hand is extended towards Kuo at waist height; his left foot is forward poised on the heel; his head is inclined a little to the left; his eyes glance right. Kuo, feet squarely together, stands facing the audience and bows over his hands, which are held together in front of him, right hand over left. The headman and the court runners go off right of the audience, followed by K'uang's assistant. K'uang turns to go after them as the curtain is drawn.*)
(*Curtain.*)

Scene 7: The Search for the Rat

The first part of the scene is played before the second curtain, the stage area representing the foot of Mount Hui near the Eastern Peak Temple. K'uang Chung's assistant comes on with Ch'in Ku-hsin. The assistant is disguised as a peddler. Ch'in Ku-hsin wears the same costume as before.

CH'IN KU-HSIN (*standing at center front stage with the disguised assistant*): After searching in all directions for several days, I've just heard that Lou the Rat is living in that thatched cottage.
(*He is facing front stage, his left hand held at waist height against the front of his body, while with his right hand lifted at face height, he points with his index finger across the heads of the audience. His right foot is squarely forward, and his left foot is poised with heel lifted and toe turned outwards. The disguised assistant, his left hand supporting his pole, his right hand held at waist height, and his feet placed squarely apart, follows the gesture of Ch'in Ku-hsin with his gaze.*)
ASSISTANT: I say, what is Lou the Rat like?
(*Ch'in does not answer but looks straight ahead.*)
CH'IN KU-HSIN: See! That looks like Lou the Rat in front. Yes, it is! It is him! I don't want him to see me—I'd better hide!
(*He exits to the right of the audience. Lou the Rat enters*

*furtively to the left of the audience. He starts when he sees
the assistant and turns back to glance at him. He is against
the curtain about three feet beyond the assistant; his knees
are slightly bent and his feet apart. His left hand is raised
in front of him at chest height; his right hand is held in front
of him below his waist. The assistant glances at Lou, shakes
his rattle, and striding past him, exits to the right of the
audience. Lou the Rat turns to face the audience, his expression half-puzzled, half-frightened. His right heel is raised,
the foot turned outwards from the left foot. He is leaning
towards the right, holding his left-hand palm open but with
fingers curled in front of him at chest height. He is pointing
before him with the index finger of his right hand, which is
above the left hand; the right arm is not fully extended.)*

LOU THE RAT (*emphasizing his words with the pointing gesture*):
Who is he? Who's that . . . Ah, a man who has done no
wrong doesn't dread a knocking on his door at night. Ever
since I came to Wuhsi, I've had no peace of mind. I can
neither sit still nor lie down quietly. For the last ten days,
I've been hiding in the country. I really cannot bear it any
more. The priest at the Eastern Peak Temple in front there
is an acquaintance of mine. He often goes into the town to
buy candles and incense. There's no help for it: I'll go and
ask him to listen for any rumors in the town; I'll ask him to
draw lots before the idol and find out whether I'll have luck
or not. (*He draws himself up. He has lowered his right arm,
but his right heel and his left hand are still in the same position. He recites in kan-pan.*)
Hiding in the country
Is an intolerable business.
When Prefect K'uang
Decides to go away,
I shall return again.
(*He faces the audience as he concludes his rhyme. He has
lowered his right heel; both his hands are raised at chest
height in front of him. With his left hand, he gestures towards
the audience, then turns and exits quickly to the right of the
audience. Ch'in Ku-hsin comes on with K'uang Chung's assistant.*)

CH'IN KU-HSIN: There he is. I'll go back first. (*He goes off.*)

ASSISTANT: Thank you. (*He peers into the distance, watching Lou the Rat going towards the temple.*) Our prefect, in disguise, has been searching high and low for days and is getting anxious, for the time is nearly up. Now that we have found Lou the Rat's hideout, he will be pleased.

(*The first court runner enters in disguise.*)

FIRST RUNNER: How is everything?

ASSISTANT: Lou the Rat is now in the Eastern Peak Temple. Go quickly and tell His Honor.

FIRST RUNNER: Let me go into the temple and arrest him.

ASSISTANT: His Honor says that although Lou the Rat is under deep suspicion, it is still not proved that he is the murderer, so we must be careful what we do. I'll keep watch here; you go back to the boat and report to His Honor. Then we'll know the right thing to do.

(*The assistant goes off right of the audience; the runner exits to the left.*)

(*The second curtain is drawn back to show the interior of the Eastern Peak Temple. Plate 9 shows the decor. The only functional property in this ornate setting is a small, plain, wooden, four-legged bench used for the main action of this scene, which is a very famous one in the Chinese repertoire. Lou the Rat appears from the rear left of the stage and stands in front of the altar screen. His knees are bent, heels together and feet turned out; both hands are held out with upturned palms at waist height.*)

LOU THE RAT: The priest has gone to town to buy incense and has not returned yet. Let me draw lots to test my luck until he comes back. Aiya! Emperor of the Eastern Peak, if all is well, reward me with a sign!

(*He bends down, his back to the audience, and draws a bamboo slip from a vase at the base of the altar.[24] Just as he*

24. In Chinese temples it was customary to have placed in a vase before the altar bamboo slips on which were written propitious sayings. Worshippers drew these at random as a token of favor from the gods before offering their prayers.

*bends down, K'uang Chung, disguised as a fortune-teller,
enters from the rear, left of the audience.*)

K'UANG CHUNG: Hey, brother!

(*He stands with his right foot placed forward and poised on
the heel. He holds his fortune-telling sign before him at
waist height with his left hand, his right hand holding his
fan out towards Lou the Rat. His head and shoulders are inclined slightly towards his left. Lou the Rat, still on his
knees, gives a startled jerk, half turning to face K'uang
Chung, his bent right arm held above his right knee. He is
sideways to the audience, leaning slightly towards his left.*)

LOU THE RAT: You made me jump! What do you want?

K'UANG CHUNG: Would you like your fortune told?

LOU THE RAT: Fortune told? No, no! I'm drawing lots here.

K'UANG CHUNG: Drawing lots is not as good as fortune-telling.

LOU THE RAT: Drawing lots is not as good as fortune-telling?

K'UANG CHUNG: Certainly not! If you have any trouble on your
mind, want to hear your luck in the future, or know your
fate, I'll make it absolutely clear for you. If you wish to
change bad luck to good luck, find anyone you are looking
for, better your affairs, or win money by gambling, let me
tell your fortune and I will enlighten you. My method is a
thousand times efficacious.

(*Putting down the bamboo slip he holds and rising, Lou the
Rat stands with feet apart, left foot slightly forward and
poised on the toe, right arm hanging down by his side, and
left arm held in front of him at waist height as he gazes at the
sign held up by K'uang Chung.*)

LOU THE RAT. Ah, you'll tell my fortune? May I ask how you
will do it?

K'UANG CHUNG: I will tell you:

(*Sings in the Hao Chieh Chieh modal pattern.*)

I do it according to the context of words.

My fame is known everywhere.

LOU THE RAT: You tell fortunes from the context of words? How
do you do that?

(*He stands with both arms held at waist height, fingers extended, and palms upturned. His feet are slightly apart, his
knees bent. K'uang Chung has moved around to the other*

side of him and stands with left foot forward a little, knee
slightly bent. He holds his right arm behind his back and his
sign up in his left hand for Lou the Rat to see.)

K'UANG CHUNG: Brother, if you have trouble on your mind, write
down any character at random, and I can decide your fate.

LOU THE RAT: You can't, you can't!

K'UANG CHUNG: Why can't I?

LOU THE RAT: Why can't you? Because I can't read or write a
single word, that's why!

(*Lou the Rat stands with his hands at chest height, wrists*
bent, extended fingers hanging down, head cocked to one
side, glancing at K'uang Chung. In fact, he looks exactly like
a rat with its paws held in midair. K'uang Chung gestures
towards Lou the Rat with his closed fan held horizontally
between the thumb and first and middle fingers of the right
hand.)

K'UANG CHUNG: Then just *tell* me one word: that will do just as
well.

LOU THE RAT: What—telling you a word will do just the same?
(*He is poised forward on the toe of his left foot, and he*
points at K'uang with the index finger of the right hand,
which is held before him at shoulder height. His left arm is
held in front of him at waist height.)

K'UANG CHUNG: Certainly. (*With his right hand, he raises his fan*
vertically to face height. His right foot is placed well forward,
his left foot placed at a right angle to it.)

LOU THE RAT: Sir, my name is Lou the Rat. The character for
rat—will that do for you?

K'UANG CHUNG: That will do, that will do!

LOU THE RAT: Let me get a bench for us.
(*He brings the wooden bench from the rear of the stage, and*
they both sit down, K'uang Chung first, crossing his left leg
over the right. Lou the Rat, on the left of the bench to the
audience, cocks his right foot up on the bench and rests his
hand on his knee.)

K'UANG CHUNG: What is it you want me to find out from this
character?
(*Lou the Rat looks furtively from right to left, then leans*
confidentially towards K'uang. His left hand, fingers ex-
tended and palm inwards, is held before his mouth as he

whispers; his whisper, needless to say, is audible to every member of the audience.)

LOU THE RAT: A court case!

K'UANG CHUNG (*turning his face towards Lou the Rat and speaking in a clear voice*): Ah, a court case!

LOU THE RAT (*terror-stricken*): S-sh! (*He turns towards K'uang Chung. His right foot slips from the bench and he holds it poised in midair, as he places his extended right hand in front of the fortune-teller's face and then slowly draws it back to hold it pawlike at shoulder height. He finally subsides on the bench again, both feet on the floor.*)

K'UANG CHUNG (*looking knowingly at Lou the Rat and emphasizing his words with his fan held in the right hand*): The character "rat" has fourteen strokes; it is an even number, that is to say, it is a dark number. The rat is also a dark animal; this is a doubly dark and obscure portent. If it is a court case, it will not be easily decided. (*While K'uang speaks, his left hand is placed on the knee of his left leg, which remains jauntily cocked over the right.*)

LOU THE RAT: Difficult to decide, but will there be trouble afterwards?

(*His head is tilted slightly towards the fortune-teller, although his eyes look front. His hands, fingers slightly curved and palms down, are held at chest height in front of him; his left leg is raised a little higher than the right and poised on the toes. K'uang Chung holds his fan vertically at chest height in line with his glance, which is directed in front of him as he speaks. His legs are still crossed; he leans slightly towards his right.*)

K'UANG CHUNG: Do you want to know this for yourself, or for somebody else?

LOU THE RAT (*glancing slyly at K'uang Chung*): Ah, ah, for somebody else, for somebody else, of course.

K'UANG CHUNG: Judging from the character, I should not think it is for somebody else.

(*Lou the Rat looks startled.*)

Ah, the rat is the source of all calamity!

LOU THE RAT: The source of the Huai River?[25]

25. There is a considerable play on word, sound, and meaning here which cannot be translated into English. K'uang Chung says in Chinese:

K'UANG CHUNG: Not the source of the Huai River, but the chief offender—the cause of the trouble.

(*Lou the Rat is terrified. He draws back from K'uang Chung, who has transferred his fan to his left hand and holds his clenched right fist forward with the thumb vertically extended. Lou the Rat's right hand, palm outwards, is drawn back to the side of his face; his left hand, with fingers curved downward, is held at waist height in front of him. His mouth gapes open, and his wide, staring eyes are directed at K'uang Chung's upraised thumb.*)

The rat is the first of the twelve cyclical animals of the Zodiac;[26] must it not, therefore, be the clue for all evil? This character indicates that you are in difficulty because you robbed a man, is that not so, brother?

(*While he is speaking, K'uang Chung looks meaningfully at Lou the Rat, inclining slightly towards him. His left hand is on his left leg, which is still cocked across the right, and the fan in his right hand is held diagonally in front of his chest. Lou the Rat, who sits facing squarely front, raises his right hand with fingers curled to chest height and opens his mouth wide in alarm again at the fortune-teller's words. He then leaps to his feet and stands about three feet from the bench. His knees and body are bent, his head turned towards K'uang Chung, and his right hand raised, with fingers extended and palm outwards, across his chest in K'uang's direction. His left hand is placed on his left thigh. K'uang Chung remains*)

Ah shu shih wei huo chih shou ni. Lou the Rat replies: *Huai ho chih shui?* Here, Lou the Rat confuses the dialectical sound pattern of *wei huo* in K'uang's statement, meaning "calamity," with *Huai ho,* a well-known river. K'uang finally answers Lou the Rat with *Pu shih Huai ho chih shui nai shih tsui k'uei huo shou;* the last two syllables mean "cause of trouble" and *tsui k'uei* is a "principal offender." This doubling of sound and meaning is characteristic of Chinese dramatic dialogue.

26. In old China the calendar was divided into twelve branches, or characters, of time, each of which was associated with a symbolic animal, a specific hour of the day, and a point of the compass. The first of the twelve branches was the character *tzu,* represented by the Rat and corresponding to Aries in Western Zodiacal terms. The corresponding hour for the Rat was the third watch, or 11 P.M. to 1 A.M., and the compass point was north. These facts lie behind the allusions made by K'uang Chung.

in the same position, eyeing Lou the Rat and raising his left hand to hold the upper end of the closed fan grasped in his right hand.)

LOU THE RAT: Sir! You wander through the markets, while I spend my time in the gambling houses. We're birds of a feather; you can't fool me, so don't try, don't try! How do you know a man was robbed?

(*Lou the Rat returns to his seat on the bench. K'uang Chung uncrosses his legs and sits with his feet wide apart. His left palm is turned upward, the hand held just above the knee, and the closed fan in his right hand is held diagonally across his face as he looks knowingly at Lou the Rat.*)

K'UANG CHUNG: The rat is an expert thief, so that's why I was able to tell.

(*Lou the Rat throws back his head and chuckles. Both hands are on his thighs. He is sitting perched on the end of the bench so that his right foot is on the floor between the front and rear legs at the side of the bench; his left foot is raised forward and off the floor with the movement of his body in laughing. K'uang Chung continues.*)

There's one more thing: wasn't the robbed man's name Yu?

(*Lou the Rat is so startled by these words that he somersaults backward over the bench and appears beneath it on his knees, with both hands placed on the floor in front of him, as he peers up furtively at K'uang Chung, who has risen to his feet. Now, as at no time before, Lou the Rat looks like a furtive rodent. When performed by a skilled comic actor, the acrobatics of Lou the Rat at this point always entrance the audience. Wang Ch'uan-sung's 1956 performance of this scene, for example, could best be described by the expression "greased lightning." K'uang Chung is standing at his side of the bench with right foot thrust forward and poised on the heel. His right hand is held forward at waist height, index and middle fingers pointing at Lou. He holds his bent left arm at shoulder height, and with his left hand, he has grasped the ends of his beard; both the beard and the folded fan, the latter grasped in the middle, are held between the thumb and first, second, and third fingers. K'uang Chung exclaims:*)

Ah, please be careful!

(*The Rat crawls from under the bench and perches himself on the bench once again. K'uang Chung has resumed his former position, his left hand on his left thigh and his right hand holding the fan, which is placed above the left hand.*)

LOU THE RAT: Look here, I told you not to try and fool me, but you're at it again. I don't believe you guessed that name. How did you guess?

K'UANG CHUNG: I followed a method of reasoning.

LOU THE RAT: What reasoning?

K'UANG CHUNG: The rat is very fond of stealing oil, isn't that so?[27]

LOU THE RAT: That's right! The rat steals oil. (*Here his left leg is raised as high as his waist. His hands, the index finger on each extended but slightly curved, are held in front of him as he mimes a rat drawing the oil container towards it. He swings around to gaze at K'uang Chung, his left leg still raised; his right hand is behind his back, while his left, still curled like a talon, is held at shoulder height to his left.*) The oil-stealing rat! (*He sits down again.*) Sir! Never mind whether it steals oil or salt—can you tell me if I am going to have trouble in the future?

K'UANG CHUNG: Of course there will be trouble. Now everything is revealed! (*He holds his folded fan between the thumb and middle finger and gestures towards Lou the Rat as he speaks. His head is inclined slightly to his right, and he is looking quizzically at his "customer."*)

LOU THE RAT (*again startled*): What do you mean?

K'UANG CHUNG: Well, you gave me the character "rat," and now it's the month of the rat. The time is here. I'm afraid this court case will soon be settled.

LOU THE RAT (*hastily glancing right and left in a nervous and confused way*): Aiya! I don't want it settled.

K'UANG CHUNG: Brother, tell me the truth! Do you want to know for yourself or for somebody else? If you answer me clearly, I can tell you a way out!

LOU THE RAT: Sir! Wait a minute!

(*He gets up, stands a few paces from the bench with his back towards K'uang Chung, and sings in the Kuei Ch'ü modal pattern.*)

27. See p. 71, n. 13.

He's there, I'm here . . .

(*He points with both hands, index fingers extended, sweeping them around to his left side, then bringing them back, palms inwards, to point at himself at chest height. He pauses, looking downwards.*)

. . . sir!

(*He turns to face K'uang Chung.*)

I am acting for . . .

K'UANG CHUNG: Ah, brother! Within the Four Seas all men are friends. Tell me whatever is worrying you; perhaps I can ease your trouble!

(*Lou the Rat goes forward, steps quickly onto the bench, and crouches close to K'uang Chung, who has opened his fan and holds it in front of his chest. With his head inclined slightly to the right, K'uang glances sideways at Lou the Rat. Lou the Rat raises his left hand, fingers extended and palm inwards, before his mouth and turns his head sideways to whisper in K'uang Chung's ear. His right hand is pressed against his chest, and his eyes are opened wide in a confidential stare.*)

LOU THE RAT: I'll be frank; I want to know my own fortune.

K'UANG CHUNG: Oh, your own fortune?

LOU THE RAT (*nervously gestures to indicate that the fortune-teller should speak more softly*): Sir, what do the stars foretell? Can I avoid trouble?

K'UANG CHUNG: Well, if you want to know your own fortune, there's nothing there.

LOU THE RAT: What do you mean?

K'UANG CHUNG: Well, if you take the top half of the character for "nothing" and add the character for "rat," don't you get the character for "furtive?"[28]

---

28. This kind of wordplay is based on the complexities of the written Chinese character, and it demonstrates the problems to be met in translating Chinese plays. Each character consists of two parts: the key character, or radical, and the phonetic. As a generalization it can be said that the radical gives a clue to the meaning of the character, and the phonetic, to its sound. There are 214 radicals, and any one of them may occupy any part of the whole character, e.g., it may be on the top, the bottom, the left, the right. The different meanings created through the juxtaposition of the different elements of the character provide the basis for this double-talk on the stage.

LOU THE RAT: What is that?

K'UANG CHUNG: It means "run away and hide."

LOU THE RAT: Sir, will I be able to run away?

(*He stands up on the bench, leaning forward, knees bent double, left foot lifted in the air, both hands raised in front of him like paws, and looks into the distance. K'uang Chung raises his eyes towards Lou the Rat and points with his right index finger across the top of the open fan, which is held in his left hand and supported against his crossed left knee.*)

K'UANG CHUNG: If you want to run away, then you certainly can. But the old rat is very suspicious by nature. If you suspect everyone right or left, not knowing whether he's a ghost or a demon, then I fear you will never make the journey. To go forwards or backwards will be equally difficult, and you'll never be able to run away.

(*Lou the Rat has now jumped down from the bench and stands behind it, leaning forward with his right hand resting on the end. His closed left hand is held at waist height; his left foot is placed well to the rear. He speaks respectfully to K'uang Chung, who sits in the same position listening, but has now closed his fan and holds it in his right hand, resting on top of his left.*)

LOU THE RAT: Sir, your powers really fulfill expectations. Lately, I've been ready to suspect everybody, as you say. I will follow your advice. When do you think is the best time for me to go?

K'UANG CHUNG: If you want to go, you must go today; by tomorrow it will not be possible.

(*Lou the Rat moves around to K'uang Chung's left and stands with his feet apart and his hands in front of his waist as he leans confidentially over the fortune-teller's left shoulder. K'uang Chung has turned his head to the left, but does not face Lou the Rat, gazing ahead instead.*)

LOU THE RAT: Why not?

K'UANG CHUNG: The top part of the character for "rat" is made from the character for "bowl," which consists of two half days; therefore, the whole meaning is one day. If you wait until tomorrow, it will be two days, and you will not be able to go.

LOU THE RAT: (*lifting his left-hand palm outwards towards K'uang*): Aiya, it's late in the day already. Tell me how to go.

K'UANG CHUNG: Well, the rat conceals itself during the day and runs about through the night: now is the very best time to go.

LOU THE RAT: Sir, may I bother you to have a look and point out the best way to go without any trouble?

K'UANG CHUNG: (*ponders a moment or two*): Wait until I think it out . . . The character for "rat" is connected with the character for "sun" of the Eight Diagrams, and "sun" is connected with "east." You should go southeast![29]

(*Lou the Rat has moved over to K'uang's right again and stands behind the bench, feet apart and leaning forward from the waist. K'uang Chung remains calmly in the same position, his closed fan held obliquely before his chest.*)

LOU THE RAT: (*emphasizing his words with his right index finger uplifted*): Southeast? Sir, may I trouble you once more to see if it's safer to go by the water or land?

K'UANG CHUNG: Wait a moment until I work it out.

(*He appears to be calculating, his head bowed over his hands, which emphasize his words with gesture. Lou the Rat has moved around to the left of the fortune-teller again and stands watching intently. His right hand is placed on the end of the bench, his bent left arm lifted at chest height.*)

"Rat" is connected with the first character of the Twelve Branches, which is connected with "water." It is best to go by water!

(*Lou the Rat crosses to the other side once more and squats*

---

29. The Chinese original here, which reads *shu shu sun, sun shu tung*, is a piece of linguistic juggling introduced for euphony and for the correct fortune-telling atmosphere. The Eight Diagrams are arrangements of single and divided lines in eight groups containing three lines each; they are often portrayed in an octagonal frame which defines the points of the compass. These diagrams originated in the classic *I Ching* and have always been the stock-in-trade of Chinese geomancers and fortune-tellers. In the jingle quoted above, the first *shu* means "rat," while the second *shu*—although identically pronounced—means "connected with" or "dependent upon." *Sun* is the character given to one of the Eight Diagram arrangements and symbolizes "southeast." *Tung* means "east." Better men than Lou the Rat might be confounded by such sorcery.

on the bench, left leg crossed over the right, his right hand grasping his left foot, and his left hand gripping the edge of the bench. He looks at K'uang Chung out of the corners of his eyes as he speaks; and K'uang Chung, in the same position as before, inclines his head and body slightly towards Lou the Rat.)

LOU THE RAT: To the southeast by water, Wuhsi, Wangting, Kuanshang, Suchou . . . (*He starts at the sound of his hometown.*)

K'UANG CHUNG: Then Chiahsing, Hangchou—Hangchou is a fine place!

LOU THE RAT: Ah, if only there were a convenient boat going southeast, I could jump aboard and sail off; that would be really good.

(*K'uang Chung rises to his feet and stands with his left foot forward and poised on the heel; his uplifted left hand holds his fan horizontally, and his right arm is outstretched at waist height towards Lou the Rat. Lou the Rat has leaped from the bench and stands bent forward from the waist, his bent left leg forward and poised on the toe, his heel lifted. His left hand is again lifted like a paw at waist height; his right arm is bent outwards from his right side, his right hand twisted to the rear from the wrist.*)

K'UANG CHUNG: I have a boat ready, brother. All being well, we sail tonight. We're going to Suchou and Hangchou to catch the New Year trade. But . . .

LOU THE RAT: I beg you, sir, take me with you. I'll pay well, I promise you!

K'UANG CHUNG: Oh, don't worry about that. It's not a question of money. Benevolence and justice are worth more than a thousand pieces of gold. But the boat may be rather slow for you. If you've no objection to that, brother, then by all means I'll take you.

LOU THE RAT: Aiya, you're not a fortune-teller! (*He goes down on his knees before K'uang with his hands placed together and raised in front of him at chest level in salutation.*)

K'UANG CHUNG (*turning to face Lou the Rat*): What?

(*His right hand, holding the closed fan, is extended towards the kneeling culprit. His bent left arm is raised before him at chest level; his left foot is placed forward in front of his right, which is at a right-angled stance to the left foot.*)

LOU THE RAT: You're a prince of saviors. I entrust my life to you.

K'UANG CHUNG: Don't worry, I'll guarantee you a safe passage!

LOU THE RAT (*rising to his feet to face the audience and singing in the Chieh Chieh Ju P'o Tiao modal pattern*):

I'm like a fish finding a hole in the net
And hurriedly escaping into the ocean.

(*His right foot is forward, and he holds his hands before him at waist level, his body and head inclined to his left. He finishes his song with both hands held up at shoulder height as he gazes rapturously upwards. His right foot is poised on the toe, heel raised. K'uang Chung stands to the left and a little to the rear of Lou the Rat. His right foot is poised on the heel.*)

K'UANG CHUNG (*joining in the song*):

I only hope your troubles will pass and luck attend you,
And that after today, all will go well.

(*He emphasizes the song with his fan, which is held vertically in his right hand; his left hand grasps the end of his beard and draws it across in a final pose.*)

LOU THE RAT (*in a final burst of song*):

I shall fly as far away as possible!

(*He stops, and turning to K'uang Chung, speaks.*) Sir, where is your boat?

(*K'uang Chung points ahead with the fan in his right hand, holding the hem of his right water sleeve with his left hand. Lou the Rat gazes toward the distant point indicated.*)

K'UANG CHUNG: Right ahead, moored by the riverbank.

(*Lou the Rat turns to face K'uang Chung, who turns also, his fan held vertically towards Lou the Rat, his bent left arm raised at waist height.*)

LOU THE RAT: I'm living in that thatched hut on the opposite bank. Here's money for your fortune-telling, and here's my fare. (*His left leg is forward, his left arm extended towards K'uang Chung, and his bent right arm raised in front of him at waist height.*) Please take it. I'm just going to get a few clothes and the rest of my cash. I'll be right back.

K'UANG CHUNG: Be quick. I'll wait for you at the boat!

(*Lou the Rat scurries offstage to the left of the audience. The court runner and K'uang Chung's assistant come on right of the audience.*)
Follow that man quickly!
(*The court runner goes off left of the audience. K'uang addresses his assistant.*)
Go back to town immediately and bring the court runners; then get all the neighbors to go and search Lou the Rat's house. If you find any suspicious article, bring it to Suchou tonight. Don't fail to do this!
(*The assistant goes off right of the audience and is shortly followed by K'uang Chung, who strides deliberately after him with the gait which has already been described.*)
(*Curtain.*)

Scene 8: The Rat Brought to Trial

The scene begins before the second curtain, the stage area representing the exterior of the Suchou prefectural court. K'uang Chung's assistant comes on soliloquizing, at the left of the audience.

ASSISTANT: I made a search as ordered. Thanks to a fair wind, I've arrived with some real evidence. (*He arrives at front center stage and stands there.*) I'm going into court now to make a statement. Yesterday, when I went to search Lou ·the Rat's house, I found a hiding place under the bed concealing several master keys and some loaded dice. There was also a bag of money which Old Ch'in swore belonged to Yu Hu-lu. If Lou the Rat wasn't the murderer, how is it that the dead man's money is in his house? Because we know Lou the Rat is crafty, Old Ch'in has volunteered to come and give evidence. (*He calls out.*) Uncle Ch'in, come quickly!
(*Ch'in Ku-hsin appears left of the audience and stands with his knees bent, hands held in front of him at waist height. The assistant, left leg forward and poised on the heel, gazes toward the right of the stage to the audience and points with*

his right hand held at chest height across his body, his left
hand held slightly below his right at waist height.)
Come with me and wait in the anteroom while I go into the
court to report to His Honor.

CH'IN KU-HSIN: Very well.

(*The two exit right of the audience. K'uang Chung enters left*
of the audience. He is in full official dress again and stands
facing the audience at center stage. His right arm is raised
at shoulder height, his left bent at chest height in front of
him. He sings in the Fen Tieh Erh modal pattern.)

K'UANG CHUNG:

We searched everywhere and in the end found the culprit.
When the tide ebbs, the rocks appear.
When the fog clears, the clouds lift.
By taking a risk and sparing no effort, I have saved two lives.
(*Speaks.*) Come! Open the Court.

(*He exits left of the audience. The second curtain is drawn*
to reveal the Suchou prefectural court. It is the same setting
as previously. There is the sound of clappers from backstage,
and a court runner comes on and places himself left of the
prefect's dais.)

RUNNER: Hey you! The third call has sounded. Records must be
sent through the main door, prisoners through the second
door. His Honor is about to take his seat in Court. Quickly,
get ready!

(*The other attendants and runners come on, followed by*
K'uang Chung's assistant, and then the prefect himself. He
takes his seat as described earlier.)

K'UANG CHUNG: Bring Su Hsü-chüan into Court!

(*The runners bring her in. She kneels before the prefect to*
the left of the audience. In front of her to the right stands a
court runner holding her father's purse extended between his
hands. The purse is a cotton strip about five feet long and
six inches wide. It has a satchel at one end into which the
strings of cash are fitted.)

K'UANG CHUNG: Su Hsü-chüan, do you recognize this purse?

SU HSÜ-CHÜAN: That is my father's purse. Why is it here?

K'UANG CHUNG: You say it is your father's: how can you prove it?

SU HSÜ-CHÜAN: My father burned a hole in it, and I mended it and embroidered a cluster of flowers over the patch. Please look for yourself, Your Honor.

K'UANG CHUNG: You may leave the Court for the time being.

SU HSÜ-CHÜAN: Yes, sir! (*She rises and is led off.*)

RUNNER (*entering*): Your Honor, there is someone from the governor to see you.

K'UANG CHUNG: Ask him to come in.

RUNNER: Sir!

(*He exits. The governor's captain of the guard enters.*)

CAPTAIN OF THE GUARD (*sarcastically*): Your humble servant!

K'UANG CHUNG: What is your business, sir?

CAPTAIN OF THE GUARD (*aggressively*): When Your Honor went to Wuhsi on investigations, the governor made it clear that you were granted two weeks only. The time is up today, and he has not yet seen your report and wants to know why. The murderers with their spoils were discovered in the Yu Hu-lu case, and the case was closed after three months. Your Honor refused to accept this, and relying on the Imperial warrant, foolishly defended the criminals and prolonged the stay of execution. You disobeyed orders from above and improperly hindered the law, and the governor has ordered you to see him at once. If investigation has proved there really was a miscarriage of justice, you may be pardoned; but if you have found nothing, you must relinquish your seal of office and await your impeachment. (*As he finishes his speech, the captain of the guard has turned his back on the prefect and faces the audience. His right arm is outstretched, first and second fingers extended; his left arm, behind him, grasps the sword at his side.*)

K'UANG CHUNG: Wait a moment, please! (*To the court runners.*) Give him a seat!

(*A chair is brought, and the captain of the guard seats himself, feet wide apart, hands at his hips.*)

K'UANG CHUNG: Bring in Lou the Rat!

(*A runner leads the cowering figure in. He goes down on his knees and makes a servile obeisance to the prefect.*)

LOU THE RAT (*very respectfully*): Your Honor!

K'UANG CHUNG (*scornfully*): You've done a fine thing!

LOU THE RAT: I've done nothing wrong!

K'UANG CHUNG: You murdered Yu Hu-lu and stole fifteen strings of cash. Do you still deny it?

LOU THE RAT (*cringing*): I am being wronged!

K'UANG CHUNG: You still say that. (*He points to the loaded dice, which are on his desk, and asks the runner to hand them to Lou the Rat.*) Give him these to look at! Are these yours?

LOU THE RAT (*looking up at the dice held out in the court runner's right hand and raising his right hand in denial*): They're not mine.

(*K'uang Chung sits up erectly on his chair, his feet placed wide apart, the toes of his boots facing right and left beneath the hem of his robe. His right hand rests on his desk; his left hand, first and second fingers extended, gestures towards Lou the Rat.*)

K'UANG CHUNG: Lift up your head.

(*Lou the Rat turns his head towards the prefect.*)

Do you recognize the fortune-teller from the temple?

(*Lou the Rat raises his left hand before his face in fear, his right hand also raised behind his left, as he cringes back.*)

Dog! Confess quickly.

LOU THE RAT (*defiantly*): First, there's no evidence; second, there are no witnesses. Your Honor would not wrong an innocent man?

K'UANG CHUNG (*lifting up the purse from his desk*): Take this and let him see it! (*To Lou the Rat.*) Do you recognize this purse?

LOU THE RAT: Where did that come from?

K'UANG CHUNG: It was found in your house; how is it that you don't recognize it?

LOU THE RAT: Oh, it's only a small thing of mine.

K'UANG CHUNG: If it's yours, is there any mark on it to prove it?

LOU THE RAT: Mark? I don't remember one.

K'UANG CHUNG: Bring in Old Ch'in.

RUNNER (*calling*): Old Ch'in into Court!

(*Ch'in Ku-hsin comes in and goes down on his knees before the prefect.*)

K'UANG CHUNG: You may stand up to speak, Old Ch'in. Lou the Rat says this purse belongs to him. What have you to say?

(*The court runner steps forward holding the purse with out-*

stretched hands and shows it to Ch'in. Lou the Rat is to the right and some distance away from the group before the prefect's dais. He is on his right knee, his right hand held paw-like in front of him. His left knee is raised with the foot squarely on the floor, and his left arm is resting on his knee. He looks anxiously towards the group examining the purse. Ch'in takes hold of the satchel end of the purse with his left hand and emphasizes his words with his outstretched right hand.)

CH'IN KU-HSIN: Lou the Rat is lying. This purse belonged to Yu Hu-lu for certain. I was his neighbor for many years and often helped him to buy pigs. I know his purse well. Last year Yu Hu-lu got drunk and burned a hole as big as your thumb in it. His daughter Su Hsü-chüan embroidered a cluster of flowers over the hole. Please look, Your Honor!

K'UANG CHUNG (*to Lou the Rat*): Dog! You're caught this time! What have you to say now?

(With his feet placed slightly apart, his left hand held in front of him just below his waist, and his right arm held against his side, Ch'in turns to look at the criminal. K'uang Chung, his head bent, glowers at Lou the Rat. Lou the Rat turns on both knees to face the audience. His right hand grasps his right thigh; his left hand is lifted to shoulder height, fingers extended and palm outwards. He leans forward, supported by his right hand; his head is tilted to his left, and he gazes upwards in desperation.)

LOU THE RAT: Ai! There's no way out. I'll confess. I did it. That night when everything was still and it was very late, I'd lost everything, not a cent left, and the door of Yu Hu-lu's shop was still open. So suddenly I stepped inside to get some pork on credit. Su Hsü-chüan was not at home and Yu Hu-lu was fast asleep. It was only to get the cash from him that I murdered him. I killed him with his own chopper and then threw suspicion on others. This is the truth, I swear. (*He slumps down, shoulders hunched, an expression of anguish on his face.*)

K'UANG CHUNG: Did you have an accomplice?

LOU THE RAT: I did it alone.

K'UANG CHUNG: Here, make him sign a confession!

(*Two runners step forward; one holds the confession for the criminal to sign, the other seizes him and forces him to sign with a writing brush. The composition and posture are the same as that described for the wrongly arrested pair earlier.*)

K'UANG CHUNG: You dog! You thieved, gambled, and committed murder. Put him in the cangue and take him off to the condemned cell. Old Ch'in, you may leave!

(*The runners lead Lou the Rat off. Ch'in goes off. K'uang Chung addresses the governor's captain of the guard, who is still seated, saying nothing.*)

Although the case was tried three times, the real criminal has only just been sentenced. Don't you think this is strange?

(*The captain of the guard looks ill at ease, but says nothing, his head still averted from K'uang Chung's gaze.*)

Bring Hsiung Yu-lan and Su Hsü-chüan into Court.

RUNNERS (*calling out one after the other*): Bring Hsiung Yu-lan and Su Hsü-chüan into Court!

(*The two are led in by the court runners and go down on their knees facing each other, that is to say, in profile to the audience. Su Hsü-chüan is to the left and Hsiung Yu-lan to the right of the audience.*)

K'UANG CHUNG: Hsiung Yu-lan and Su Hsü-chüan, the real murderer, Lou the Rat, has confessed, so your innocence is proved. (*To the runners.*) Take the chains off these two!

(*The court runners remove the chains.*)

Stand up, Hsiung Yu-lan. Here are your fifteen strings of cash. Take them back.

(*The runner offers the money to Hsiung Yu-lan; he is so overjoyed that he forgets to take the cash.*)

Su Hsü-chüan, here are ten taels of silver for you. You may now go to your aunt in Kaoch'iao.

(*The girl is so overcome that she too forgets her money. Both the man and the girl go down on their knees before the prefect. Su Hsü-chüan is nearer to the audience, with her back to it. Hsiung Yu-lan is nearer to the prefect and in half profile to the audience. They cry out in unison, the girl with her hands clasped before her face, Hsiung Yu-lan with arms outstretched towards the prefect.*)

HSIUNG YU-LAN AND SU HSÜ-CHÜAN: Oh, honored sir!

(They sing in duet in the Huang Lung Kun modal pattern.)
Your Honor is like a bright crystal lamp,
A precious mirror that sees everything,
Shedding light everywhere.
You are like the great iron-faced judge Pao Ch'eng.
(The runners hand Hsiung the money again.)
But for Your Honor's great righteousness,
We should have been wronged spirits executed unjustly.
We should have been executed unjustly;
We would not be alive today!

K'UANG CHUNG: You may go!

HSIUNG YU-LAN AND SU HSÜ-CHÜAN *(together)*: Our most grateful
appreciation. A thousand thanks, Your Honor, for saving our
lives!

*(They rise and turn to go but draw back as the governor's
captain of the guard steps forward. Su Hsü-chüan is the
nearer to him. She pauses, leaning to the left, her bent left
arm held outwards with fingers as described on p. 22; her
right arm is across her chest and her right leg behind the
left leg poised on the toes. Hsiung Yu-lan has lifted both
hands to his waist, the left hand holding the strings of cash;
his left foot is forward and turned; his whole body is inclined
slightly backwards and to the left. The captain of the guard
bars their way with outstretched left arm.)*

CAPTAIN OF THE GUARD: Not so fast! We cannot let them go before
reporting to the governor!

K'UANG CHUNG *(rises to his feet)*: I have set free two wrongly
accused murderers, and in return, provided him with a real
murderer. What is there to fear? *(To the hesitant couple.)*
You may go!

(The two hasten to the entrance.)

SU HSÜ-CHÜAN *(turning to Hsiung Yu-lan)*: Sir, I involved you
in all this . . .

HSIUNG YU-LAN: Don't say that. It's all the fault of that stupid
magistrate Kuo. Why should you be blamed? Come on, let's
go.

SU HSÜ-CHÜAN: Let's go.

(They exit together.)

CAPTAIN OF THE GUARD (*turning to face the audience with arms held wide, palms upwards, fingers extended*): An admirable prefect, really. Your Honor set an unjust sentence right. It does you merit.
(*K'uang Chung has stepped down before the captain of the guard. His heels are together, feet turned outwards; his left hand grips his jade girdle; his right-hand fingers are curled, thumb extended towards the governor's officer. The captain stands with left foot placed forward, hands clasped in front of him at his waist, leaning forward slightly, his head lowered.*)

K'UANG CHUNG: Although I deliberately sided with the accused couple and held up the execution, at any rate the case is settled, and I have not exceeded my time limit, which is now up. We will go and report together. After you, sir!

CAPTAIN OF THE GUARD: Indeed! Indeed! Indeed!

(*Curtain.*)

THE END

Index

Other books from Wisconsin

SAN-CH'Ü: Its Technique and Imagery. By Wayne Schlepp.
". . . breaks new ground by a detailed analysis of the technique used in the *san-ch'ü* poetry of the Yüan dynasty . . . a valuable contribution to the understanding of a genre hitherto neglected by scholars writing in English. It is hoped that Professor Schlepp may follow it up with a book of more translations from *san-ch'ü*." —*Asian Affairs.* "Strongly recommended for libraries with holdings in Chinese literature . . ." —*Choice*
160 pages   1970   cloth $6.50

STAGECRAFT FOR NONPROFESSIONALS. By F. A. Buerki.
Some significant changes in approximately 30 per cent of the text make this immensely popular handbook even more valuable to all amateur theater craftsmen. ". . . rigidly scaled to the needs of the beginning amateur whose first need is one workable way of getting the show on . . . Emphasis is on realism, simplicity, and economy." —*Quarterly Journal of Speech.* ". . . extremely valuable . . . well-illustrated and well-written."—*Library Journal*
144 pages, 81 illus.   3d ed. 1972   paper $2.50

THE BROKEN WORLD OF TENNESSEE WILLIAMS. By Esther Merle Jackson. "This book is the most thoroughly competent critical appraisal of the major characteristics of the dramatic form of the inimitable Tennessee Williams . . . In seven sparsely documented but provocative chapters, she traces the remarkable growth of Williams' dramatic form from its early stages of development in the antirealist mode to a recent maturity of poetic style." —*Quarterly Journal of Speech*
208 pages, 5 illus.   1965   paper $2.50

OPERA—DEAD OR ALIVE: Production, Performance, and Enjoyment of Musical Theatre. By Ronald E. Mitchell. The author, speaking from forty years of theatre experience, is convinced that theatregoers can demand — and get — better musical theatre. Mitchell here seeks to give his reader a deeper understanding of all musical theatre, enhancing his appreciation and sharpening his critical faculties, in viewing the broad expanse of musical theatre from classical Greece to present-day America.
344 pages, 21 plates, 5 figs.   1970   cloth $12.50; paper $2.95

Other books from Wisconsin

ENDEAVORS OF ART: A Study of Form in Elizabethan Drama. By Madeleine Doran. ". . . the general reader as well as the specialist will be pleased to encounter a freshness and vitality that wears its scholarship lightly, and few will not be the wiser for having read this book." —*Times Literary Supplement.* "At the hands of a scholar at once so learned and so scrupulous as Dr. Doran, we find ourselves prepared to accept guidance through the perplexities of this difficult field." —*Shakespeare Quarterly*
496 pages, illus.   1954; reprint 1972   paper $2.95

SHAKESPEARE IN WARWICKSHIRE. By Mark Eccles. ". . . he has carefully examined the manuscript sources and gives here his interpretation of the evidence . . . The most remarkable feature of the volume is the enormous amount of detail marshalled by Professor Eccles concerning Shakespeare's background, his neighbours, his schoolfellows, his wife, and his friends . . . will be interesting for its detail and valuable as a work of reference." —*Canadian Modern Language Review.*
192 pages, 4 illus., 2 maps   1961   cloth $6.50; paper $1.75

JONSON AND THE COMIC TRUTH. By John J. Enck. ". . . all students of Jonson will be grateful for so careful a study, so filled with concrete observation and thought, and so suggestive of direction for further inquiry." —*Modern Language Quarterly.* ". . . the book has the great merit of turning one back to the plays with new interest and insight and with all the old joy." —*Modern Philology.* ". . . combines fresh appreciation, insight, and alert scholarship." —*Seventeenth-Century News*
296 pages   1957   paper $2.95

THE MORAL VISION OF JACOBEAN TRAGEDY. By Robert Ornstein. ". . . examines the ethical viewpoints and artistic achievements of all the dramatists who made significant contributions to early seventeenth-century tragedy . . . a thought-provoking book, and in its brave attempt to produce a synthesis of the various and often conflicting moods and temperaments of the period with which it deals can be sure of a warm reception." —*The Year's Work in English Studies*
310 pages   1960   paper $3.25

Other books from Wisconsin

JOHN FORD AND THE TRADITIONAL MORAL ORDER. By Mark Stavig. This study traces the relationship of early seventeenth-century ethical thought to the apparently licentious tone of Ford's plays. The early prose works as well as the plays are re-evaluated with a view toward establishing Ford's position within the framework of his time. "A new interpretation, packed with insight . . . this book contains a liberal education in several aspects of seventeenth-century drama." —*CEA Critic*
246 pages   1968   cloth $8.50

BERNARD SHAW & THE ART OF DESTROYING IDEALS: The Early Plays. By Charles A. Carpenter. ". . . his critical categories make sense, his scholarship is meticulous and the resulting analyses are full of illumination . . . Carpenter provides the best accounts we have to date of Shaw's moral psychology and of his theory of comedy, and he utilizes Shaw's own comments on his plays and the subjects they deal with far more completely than anyone has before." —*Shaw Review*
274 pages   1969   cloth $10.00

KAFKA AND THE YIDDISH THEATER. By Evelyn Torton Beck. "The thesis of this scholarly and enjoyable study is that Kafka's work was not only strongly influenced by the Yiddish plays he saw in Prague in 1911 and 1912, but also that his later dramatic style and even his themes were a direct result of his enthusiastic response to this Yiddish theater . . . fascinating literary research . . . will have a profound effect on Kafka studies . . . Highly recommended for literature collections." —*Library Journal*
270 pages   1971   cloth $12.50

THE PLAYWRIGHT AND HISTORICAL CHANGE: Dramatic Strategies in Brecht, Hauptmann, Kaiser, and Wedekind. By Leroy R. Shaw. In an engaging and fresh approach, Professor Shaw analyzes four German dramas of the turbulent 1890-1925 era, each linked by a thematic concern with change, as to their concept of reality and their varying responses to its demands. And in doing so, he skillfully places the dramas within their historical context.
194 pages   1970   cloth $6.50

Other books from Wisconsin

WE MURDERERS: A Play in Three Acts. By Gudmundur Kamban. Vi Mordere, translated from the Danish by Einar Haugen. Introduction by D. E. Askey. ". . . an extremely skillfully written play, filled with unrelenting tension, free from digressions, yet rich in nuances and psychological insights, especially regarding the feminine psyche . . . it is among the best received of his works and one of the best written Icelandic plays to date." —*Atlantica & Icelandic Review*
100 pages   1970   cloth $7.50

FIRE AND ICE: Three Icelandic Plays. Edited by Einar Haugen. *The Wish (Galdra-Loftur)* by Jóhann Sigurjónsson, translated by Einar Haugen. *The Golden Gate (Gullna hlidid)* by David Stefánsson, translated by G. M. Gathorne-Hardy. *Atoms and Madams (Kjarnorka og kvenhylli)* by Agnar Thórdarson, translated by Einar Haugen. "A stimulating glimpse into Icelandic drama for readers interested in world theater." —*The Booklist*. ". . . an important book, highly readable." —*American Notes & Queries*
274 pages   1967   cloth $5.95

CELESTINA: A Play in Twenty-One Acts Attributed to Fernando de Rojas. Translated by Mack Hendricks Singleton, with a survey of Celestina studies in the twentieth century and a selected bibliography by Cándido Ayllón. ". . . the English translation that best expresses the ribald and the earthly elements together with the sentimentality and the tenderness that are the very essence of the *Tragi-Comedy of Calisto and Melibea*." —*Arizona Quarterly*
316 pages   1958   paper $2.95

LA VIDA DE LAZARILLO DE TORMES Y DE SUS FORTUNAS Y ADVERSIDADES. (Text in Spanish.) Edited by Everett W. Hesse and Harry F. Williams. Introduction by Américo Castro. ". . . students are introduced to the flavor of sixteenth century Spanish, without being left to stumble over the unfamiliar forms . . . Teachers may welcome this opportunity for an excursion into the history of the Spanish language . . . handsome and carefully prepared edition." —*Hispania*
104 pages   1961   paper $1.50